Aphid In My Eye

by Tom Powell

Illustrations by Betsy West

Adventures

in the

Orchid Trade

B. B. Mackey Books, Wayne, PA

Text © Copyright 2012 by Thomas Powell

Cover art and line drawings © Copyright 2012 by Betsy West

ISBN 1-893443-51-5
ISBN 978-1-893443-51-8

Library of Congress CIP pending

TABLE OF CONTENTS

Once, during my 25 years in pursuit of a professional green thumb I was crying—or perhaps I was laughing 'til I cried. A colleague, a venerable wise Italian, tried to comfort me by gently asking, "Whatsa matter, you got a aphid in your eye?"

~~~ Betty Powell

Dedicated to Betty Powell, who was brave beyond the call of booty, wise to every crack, and a joy to all who knew her.

Chapter 1

Plunging Into Paradise

Chlorophyll in the veins. Some of us have it; the rest must make do with red or blue blood. You may have heard that green blood manifests itself only in the thumbs, but in the most blessed it courses through the whole body. At its greenest, it makes its possessor the royalty of the horticultural world.

Not royalty in the usual sense (though I seem to recall the "Pomp and circumstance March" playing in my head at the inauguration of a certain orchid society president). In our case, any resemblance to such exalted status was certainly not detectable. In dress, manner, and means, we were just ordinary people.

But we GREW ORCHIDS.

We not only grew orchids, we lived orchids. We jungle-ized our home, pauperized our bank accounts, and frayed and frazzled our psyches. The first flower on a newly acquired plant made us weak in the knees, and we tended to babble piteously at the sight of a bud peeping from a sheath.

We talked orchids day and night, and the few friends we had left recommended tranquilizers or a vacation in the Arctic (to which we replied, "Did you know that there are five species of orchids native to the Arctic?" and promptly described them in detail; this invariably lost us another friend).

What brought an otherwise reasonably sane twenty-something couple to this sorry state? I must warn you that what I am about to tell you will chill your blood, be it red, blue or tinted a healthy green.

It comes from the jungle, and no one has ever seen it. The world's greatest psychiatrists have studied the malady it brings, but they know only that anyone suffering from it cannot, by any means yet known to science, be cured.

Invisible even to the electron microscope, the orchid bug bites insidiously but always fatally. It invests every orchid, and one need only be given an orchid plant, or buy one on impulse because "it has such funny flowers." From that moment, there is no stopping it. It infects brain, blood, bone and marrow, and like lemmings, we leap the cliff to eternal discontent. Life becomes a quest for just one or one hundred more orchids.

As Mr. Dickens would have said, it is the best of addictions, and the worst of addictions, and it brings one to great wisdom and great foolishness.

Full House

Picture a young couple, not long married, and as average as everything else was back in the pleasantly dozing days of the 1950s. Tom and Betty Powell lived in a large apartment on Second Avenue in the Yorkville section of Manhattan's East side. The building was a four-story tenement which had been remodeled to make one apartment on each floor.

Our second floor apartment actually belonged to Betty's father. Rudy was away most of the year installing elevators from Rochester to Rio. So we were alone to enjoy the delicious miasma arising from the Italian restaurant-pizzeria on the ground floor, owned by our landlord, known fondly as Papa Pasta. After a while, we barely noticed this appetizing aroma, but when we went to dinner at some friends' houses, they were apt to sniff us and suddenly become chagrined that they were serving prime ribs instead of scaloppini.

We happily plied our trade of writing and editing garden magazines and books (our arteries were already pumping green corpuscles). And in the four big windows that faced west on Second Avenue, we grew plants, plants and more plants.

Our indoor gardens were eclectic, with pots of lettuce flourishing amid cacti, gloxinias nestling among those charming trees that sprout from avocado pits and grapefruit pips, and cherry tomatoes cascading from baskets. At the rear of the apartment, on the setback over the pizzeria's kitchen, Betty grew lilies. She didn't just grow them, she caressed and coaxed them to produce gigantic masses of flowers. Bright and overpoweringly fragrant blooms towered on tall stalks rising from huge bulbs in tin pots. The backyard neighbors cheered them on from their rear windows, except for one codger who complained that they took him back to his boyhood when is family lived next door to a funeral parlor.

Then it happened. We were managing a trade booth for *Organic Gardening Magazine* at the International Flower Show. Today, as everyone knows, *Organic Gardening* is the beacon that guides all gardeners to safe and sane gardening. In those days, it was a flickering candle bravely jousting with great clouds of DDT and ammonium nitrate.

For twelve hours a day, we were answering questions about strange things like compost, which nobody had ever heard about before. Most of the questions were intelligent, a few were disconcerting. One that was both was asked by a dowager of uncertain age but very certain height and haughtiness. She wanted to know what she should do with a truckload of organic material her husband had given her on their anniversary. When I asked her what this material was, she reared up and bellowed, "Chicken shit, my good man! Chicken shit!"

We instantly became the celebrities of the day, and we sold slews of subscriptions to hordes who apparently had or hoped to have steaming piles of odoriferous offal dumped on their front lawns.

All this was watched with avid interest by the elderly couple who were selling house plants in the booth next to ours. At the end of the show when we were packing up, Betty bought several of their plants which had caught her eye. They threw in an orchid plant.

It was an old overgrown cattleya, one of the "florist's orchids" whose flowers were used ad nauseam for prom corsages. Like so many other orchids, it was an ungainly, thoroughly unlovely plant. Betty tucked it into one of our window gardens among taller plants that would hide its ugly bulbs and long thick leaves.

But there was something about it. It had several buds, and when these opened to big purple flowers, even I had to admit that they were, well, different. All the other flowers around them seemed to fade, their colors becoming insipid, their forms turning common and not very interesting.

We began sneaking breaks from our work to watch each bud unfolding. When we noticed new growths appearing at the base of the bulbs; we threw out the plants around it so our orchid would get all the sun.

Half a dozen more orchid plants were soon acquired from a local florist. They were shockingly expensive, but we agreed that it was perfectly possible to survive for months on pizza and pasta. The second-hand book dealer who supplied us with books for our work was pestered until he produced a stream of book on orchids. More and more of our "common" plants were given to friends, and Betty's beloved lilies went out to the curb with a sign saying "Take me home." Although the price of gasoline had just gone up to 23 cents a gallon, we made trips to any and every commercial greenhouse that grew orchids within a hundred miles.

Our windows began to overflow with mini to monster cattleya flowers, long golden sprays of dancing-ladies (*oncidiums*), arching spikes of pure white flowers on the "ideal house plant" moth orchid (*phalaenopsis*), and the vivid pouch-lipped flowers of the lady-slipper orchid (*paphiopedilum*). Betty was apt to buy a plant just because it had a "musical" name. Who wouldn't want to be able to say, "My *Cyrtidiorchis stumpflei* is blooming even better this year than my *Neocogniauxia hexaptera*."

We were working far into the night every day of the week to support our orchid mania. But this was not the major problem. We were running out of room.

Let There Be (Artificial) Light

Papa Pasta became hysterical when we proposed building a greenhouse on the roof, so we could only expand inward. This meant we had to surmount a major hurdle: most orchids need lots of light, and the sun did not seep more than a few feet into any of our rooms.

Why not make our own light? We had heard that people were growing plants under fluorescent lights, so we bought one of the new lighted plant carts. The one we chose had three shelves on a frame of gleaming aluminum tubing, with fluorescent fixtures mounted above each shelf. It was handsome in a kind of high-tech way, and Betty thought it would look smashing alongside her Louis XV credenza.

Lighting for plants was primitive back then; today there are high-intensity lamps that outshine the midday sun in the Sahara. But our glow-cart worked. We became adept at arranging the plants so that each got the right amount of light. Those needing the most light went under the center of the tubes where it was brightest, and tiny plants were raised up on inverted pots so they almost touched the tubes. Any plant that dared fail to bloom with all this loving attention was sent back to the windows in disgrace.

Soon we had four glow-carts, and our "office" became The Orchid House. Our desks were turned into potting benches, and one end of the room was curtained off to hide bags of potting mixes and fertilizer. A hose attached to the kitchen faucet snaked through four rooms so we could water the plants without hauling buckets. The rug in the orchid room was replaced with linoleum that could be – and had to be – mopped frequently. We didn't even begrudge the twice-a-year repainting necessitated by the water blisters and slime that formed on the walls due to the high humidity the orchids needed.

Our orchid house delighted visitors, both two-legged and four-pawed. My back often ached from assisting a portly lady to rise after she had gotten to her knees to see that cute little plant on the bottom shelf of Orchid Garden Number Three. Our English bulldog would wag her stubby corkscrew tail as she bent her Churchillian head to sniff a lady-of-the-night (a courtesan of orchids, *Brassavola nodosa*, which had ghostly white flowers that are fabulously fragrant in the evening).

We had our Eden of orchids. But no Eden, it seems, is complete without a lurking serpent. A nagging sense of discontent, of goals unfulfilled and joys not experienced, began to slither in. There were thousands of orchids we had not yet grown, millions of flowers we had not birthed. We needed more space, more sun, and more, more, more orchids.

Betty always said (she had an "I always said..." for every situation), "Providence provides." And once again, Providence came through for us.

We Meet Our Fate

One of our favorite haunts was an orchid nursery in southwestern Connecticut. Birst & Borpling was worth the long trip because it had the biggest collection of uncommon orchids in the country. Its owners, both ancestral and current, were said to be something of a legend, though we were never told why.

One beautiful September day, we trekked to B&B. Since we were in the early withdrawal stages of a twelve-step program for orchid addiction, we had sworn to each other that we would limit ourselves to buying just three plants.

A few hours later, Albert Andrew Borpling himself sauntered out of his office to tally up or 27 purchases. As always, he had a big smile for us. The Powells were his favorite customers (as was anyone who bought more than one plant). We also had a special fascination to him: we grew orchids in the house. We were pioneers, opening a new frontier that might turn out to be a lucrative market for B&B orchids.

Albert himself was a legend in the orchid world.

In a fraternity characterized by a spirit of competitiveness not seen since the gladiators and lions, this was a man respected, no, revered, by all.

The most lovable of men, he was also the most knowledge-able when it came to orchids. He knew the provenance (where it came from) of at least 77.5 per cent of the 25,000-plus species, and every story (not always tellable in mixed company) about every orchid hunter and collector since Adam (it was not an apple, Albert revealed, but an oncidium that Eve gobbled in the Garden of Eden). To be entertained by "the great man" was a nirvana aspired to by the humblest to the most royal orchidist.

Albert always remembered every plant we had ever bought from him, and usually inquired solicitously about its health. This time, however, his queries seemed directed more towards us than to the well-being of our plants. He wanted to know where and how we lived, what we wanted to do, and (this seemed most important) did we have the money to do it with.

He finally came to the point. "Well, now, you know, I could use some good people around here. How would you like to live here and run this little place?"

We gaped at him. Providence, I thought, couldn't possibly provide this well. We had about 400 plants at home, and here were 40,000 awaiting our tender ministrations.

Seeing that we needed to sit down, Albert invited us into his office. We sat, refusing the cigars he offered both of us but accepting water glasses brimming with bourbon.

Albert said he could only pay us a small weekly salary (the word minuscule didn't seem to be in his vocabulary). But we could live free in the house adjoining the office. We would have eight hours off every second Sunday, and our nights would be free except for a little attention to the boiler, greenhouse vents, and other minor "security measures." And of course, we would have the prestige of managing world-renowned Birst & Borpling, which had been many connoisseurs' delights with the finest orchids since just after the Civil War.

We needed only a few bourbon-buoyed seconds to say yes. In less than a week, we moved ourselves and everything we owned into B&B. Our furniture was ensconced in the house beside the greenhouses, our glow-carts glowed brightly in the hospitality/packing room next to the office to show visitors how to grow orchids in their living rooms, and our plants had returned to the place where they had been born.

The old saying that dreams come true was apparently true. Unfortunately, no sage has ever amended it to warn that dreams sometimes turn into nightmares.

11

Have a cigar!

Chapter 2

Getting To Know You

The great house of Birst & Borpling Orchids, we discovered early on, was not exactly thriving. In truth, it was barely surviving, and that more because of its staff than because of its owner.

For more than 30 years, the head (and only) grower, Patsy Ruggiero, has been the rock upon which B&B squatted. Patsy's command post was the potting shed, from which he sallied forth once a day to check every plant in every greenhouse. This took him only a few minutes. His one good eye could spot a plant which needed repotting from 50 feet away. He'd stick a big red label on it so his "boys" could bring it to the potting shed later, then he'd continue loping through the greenhouses.

Patsy was a short Paul Bunyan, at least on one side. The biceps of his right arm were so massive his other arm looked withered in comparison. This overdevelopment was the result of jamming chunks of osmunda fiber – which resembled Brillo pads on steroids – into pots, hour after hour, day after day. Patsy never shook hands with people, because he could crush fingers better than a ten-ton press.

He also had instincts any weather forecaster would have given his anemometer to possess. One glance at the skylight over the potting shed and he would bark to one of the boys, "Lower the vents two inches in section four of the mountain house." Rocco or Gregory would quick-march to do his bidding (no one ever ambled when Patsy gave an order), and presto, perfection was restored in the environment of section four of the mountain house.

Patsy's chief assistant, Rocco, was the runt of the B&B litter, but he made up for his lack of stature with almost excessive strength and the reflexes of an emu. Rocco could leap the length of the potting shed and catch a falling pot before it was halfway to the floor. His great ambition was to drive racing cars, and his yearning for Le Mans inspired a hot rod approach to every task. I

Patsy (Popeye)

remember asking him one day to drop off our car for servicing at the dealership next to his house on his lunch break. It was only half a mile down the road, but Rocco got a ticket for doing 80 in a 30-mile-per-hour zone.

Second assistant, Gregory, on the other hand, was tall and handsome, a sort of black-haired, black-eyed and black-clad captain of cavalry. His father and pregnant mother had fled the purge of Stalinland, and Gregory had entered the world in the wilds of Connecticut. But he never forgot his heritage. He saluted when spoken to, and wore military boots which he polished religiously before leaving work each day. His real name was Gregorovich, and he tolerated being addressed as Gregory. Calling him Greg, Patsy warned us, might well evoke a challenge to a duel.

Patsy, Rocco and Gregory made a great team. They kept B&B running like a perpetual motion machine, with every orchid humming and blooming contentedly.

Every afternoon at two o'clock, we all got together in the potting shed for a break. Patsy made very potent coffee, Betty baked cake or cookies, and Albert was left to man the phone and practice pest control (Patsy's term for waiting on customers).

One afternoon soon after our arrival, the talk in the potting shed turned to the future. Patsy asked, "So you gonna sell lotsa plants?"

We were gonna do just that, we assured him. Interrupting each other frequently, we described our plans for a new mail-order catalog and an advertising campaign that would make Birst & Borpling not only a greenhousehold word, but bring orchids into living rooms from Boston to Burbank. Our new motto, "Orchids Bring Happiness!" would resound throughout the land, and the town would have to build an airport to bring in the masses of drooling happiness seekers hastening to B&B from every hamlet.

Oddly, our enthusiasm didn't seem to be contagious. Patsy smiled sort of half-heartedly as he picked up his fifth piece of cake, and Rocco's and Gregory's mouths twitched into pale semblances of grins.

Patsy's smile – well, it couldn't possibly be condescending, I thought, but it did seem to have overtones of Hamlet contemplating the slings and arrows, etc. Nobody cheered or raised their coffee cups in salute to our great vision. Nobody spoke, until Patsy looked up at the clock and announced, "Let's get back to work!"

As we were leaving, I turned back to tell everyone that Betty was making strudel for the next day's coffee break. All three of them were shaking their heads solemnly. Maybe they didn't like strudel, I thought.

Over Our Heads

We had decided on that very afternoon we would get started on "the books." The sooner we mastered Albert's undoubtedly very efficient system of record keeping, billing, shipping and so on, the sooner we could get to our real job bringing happiness to millions of would-be and should-be orchidists.

On our previous visit to the office, we had barely glanced around. I think we were a little awed by Albert's giant roll top desk, which Sothebys would have listed on the first page of its catalog with a string of zeroes in the minimum bid price. Albert's chair was equally impressive; a tilting and swiveling behemoth of cracked leather, with its seat embellished with one of those cute fuzzybutt pillows made for hemorrhoid suffers. There was another desk and several old oak filing cabinets, and one of the first Remingtons ever made perched on a little typewriter table.

Actually, these venerable furnishings were a little hard to see. Every horizontal surface was piled with papers. Everywhere we looked, mini-mountains of paper rose like islands thrust up by undersea volcanoes.

Albert had intimated that he was "a little over my head." Miles under was more like it. I suggested we get a shovel and a peck of plastic garbage bags, but Betty said we might learn a lot about the business and even find some sources of income in the mess.

So we waded (literally) into the piles. The sun set, but we labored on, and by dawn we had reduced 15 piles to 15 piles, but they were organized piles. One contained requests for catalogs, two were marked general correspondence, four held unfilled orders and the rest consisted of complaints from customers about unfilled orders and letters from customers' lawyers about unfilled orders.

Back in the third grade, I had a teacher who made her class stand each morning and recite three times, "If it's worth doing, it's worth doing right." Albert's version of this was, "It's only worth doing if it's fun." He never did anything that wasn't fun, and his idea of fun was to talk, and talk, and talk.

His working day consisted of strolling into the office after the mailman had come, opening the letters, and removing the checks. The latter were carefully entered into a ledger and on deposit slips for the bank. His most arduous day was the second Friday of the month, when he had to fortify himself with two breakfasts before he could make out the payroll checks for Patsy and the boys, and most painful of all, pay a few bills to keep water, electricity and fuel oil flowing into Birst & Borpling.

Then it was talk show time. Off he went to amble through the greenhouses. Spying an audience, he would activate his force field of charm. No troops liberating a city were greeted with greater joy; no guest at the Ritz was made to feel more welcome.

Albert's appearance didn't detract from his aura of benevolence. He was tall, a good six inches above my nearly six feet, and his physique was not really gaunt, but more what you would call "spare." His white hair went beyond spare to sparse. Though equally wispy, his mustache was more distinguished, being that shade of coppery gold which can be achieved only by daily dyeing with the smoke of numerous cheap cigars. His craggy countenance beamed "Bless you, my children," one and all.

This hybrid of Gandhi and an emaciated Jimmy Stewart had a prodigious knowledge of orchids and a tale to go with every plant. He would point out a particularly ugly flower that was a favorite food of the world's largest boa constrictor, or the dainty little flower that ate the giant ants which had almost cost him a leg on one of his expeditions to Bolivia. (According to Patsy, Albert had never been south of northern Alabama).

His repertoire included a soliloquy on the bee orchid. The flowers of this orchid looked exactly like inebriated bumblebees. Albert would pick up the plant and say, "Don't you just love the raw sexuality of this orchid? I have seen many a real bee trying to copulate with these flowers. To bee or not to bee. Nature is just like people – she never missed a chance to be fruitful and multiply." Maidens blushed, matrons tittered, and gentlemen smirked as they dug deep into their pockets to buy this must-have orchid.

Cyps Ahoy!

Albert was a salesman of the old school, the old old snake oil school. He possessed talents that would have been the envy of every merchant in the bazaars of Alexandria. Moreover, through a quirk of astigmatism in one eye, he always knew exactly how much he could extract from a customer. When he closed his right eye, the left on developed a kind of x-ray vision that could penetrate a purse or wallet a hundred yards away.

Both of Albert's eyes, however, were always focused on The Deal. One big deal could fill his coffers for months and swell his ego with Machiavellian glee.

The affair of the cyps was our first introduction to Albert's genius of The Deal. Cypripediums, the lady's slipper orchids which taxonomists insist should be called paphiopedilums, have flowers which are better described as handsome rather than pretty. They have three wavy or recurving petals with bright stripings or specklings, and a big bulging pouch lip. More than any other orchid, they have "substance" — petals and pouch appear to be crafted of steel-reinforced wax that makes each flower stand tall and proud for months.

Breeders had long slavered over cyps and slaved to make them bigger and better. They reasoned that a three-inch bloom would be much better if it was six inches, maybe even eight or ten inches across. One of these breeders was a special friend of Albert's.

When Bert called, Albert would huddle over the phone, cup his hand around it, and speak in whispers. Then, a few days later, a big truck would arrive, and a Big Deal was on.

The first time we witnessed this intriguing phenomenon, the Flogle truck spewed forth several dozen potted plants swathed in many layers of tissue paper. These went into one of the greenhouses, and Albert immediately posted a sign that proclaimed, "Danger! Do not enter! House being fumigated—DEADLY POISON."

Do not enter!

Albert returned to the office, but not to put on the rubber suit and air tank that had to be worn when applying pesticides. He rummaged in the back of a filing cabinet drawer and came up with a little black bag, like those that doctors carry on house calls. We deduced that these plants needed special medical treatment rather than the usual delousing given to newcomers.

A while later, we went out and peeked in at the door of the greenhouse. Dr. Albert was performing intricate surgical procedures on a group of cypripediums. These were no ordinary cyps. Their flowers looked to be almost a foot across, and they were as brilliantly hued as Time Square at midnight.

They did have one minor fault. The word "substance" was unknown to them. They flopped. They just hung from their stems, sagging like frogs exhausted from swimming the English Channel.

The rules for exhibiting orchids allow a very small amount of staking and wiring to support and position flowers so they look their best. Dr. Albert's ministrations were far more sophisticated. With bits of wire, plastic strips and cotton balls, he fashioned and installed crutches, collars and cummerbunds that made the flowers snap smartly to attention. Once it passed inspection, each bloom was carefully sprayed with what appeared to be a fixative designed to prevent it from collapsing to its normal state.

When Albert came back to the office after nearly six hours in the operating room, his face wore a broad, mustache-twisted smile. The smile broadened even more when he hung up the phone after another hand-over-mouth call. He beamed at us, announced that "Mr. Cranston of Cranston's Epicurean Victuals will be here in the morning", and departed, humming the "Triumphal March" from Aida.

We had no time to ponder this mystery, as we barely noticed when Mr. Cranston of Cranston's Epicurean Victuals arrived and in due course left with the cyps, now minus props and wires. But Betty was curious, and she checked the ledger as soon as Albert went home. There was a single entry in Albert's elegant script: "Cranston, 30 Cypripedium 'Blowsy Girl', $20,000."

We discussed this over our usual supper of crusts and surplus cheese. I suggested that next year at cypripedium blooming time, we either arrange to be out of the country or install bulletproof glass in the office windows. Betty was more pragmatic. She recommended that we hit up Albert for a substantial raise in return for taking the Fifth Amendment when Cranston vs. Birst & Borpling came up in court.

But maybe, she said, we were worrying about nothing. Surely a brain that could conceive and execute one of the greatest horticultural coups of the century should be able to deal with the consequences.

She was right. When Albert ambled in the next morning, she asked him what he intended to do when Cranston's Epicurean Victuals complained that his Blowsy Girls were producing limp dishrags instead of flowers.

"Well, now," he mused, "we'll just have to find out what he's doing wrong, won't we? He's growing them too warm, or too wet, or maybe he doesn't have enough calcium in his fertilizer. I can think of a dozen things he might not be doing right. We'll just have to correct one or two each year, and by the fifth or sixth year he'll decide to grow carnations.

"Some people," he sighed, "just don't know how to grow orchids. But it doesn't really matter, as long as they can afford to try."

Urns for Ernie

Another Flogle-Borpling collaboration was even more profitable.

Fred Flogle had "connections." One of these informed him that an estate in the Berkshires was being demolished to make way for a golf course. Its Italianate gardens contained urns, hundreds of urns, of lead, marble, bronze, terra cotta and everything else capable of being molded and sculpted. Some were squat, others were statuesque, and all were adorned with exquisite carvings of barely clad maidens and stalwart youths exchanging passionate looks and bunches of grapes.

Those priceless urns

These were free for the taking, and Fred took them. A fleet of trailer trucks delivered them to B&B one morning, and by dinner time the field next to the parking lot was filled with urns (Patsy called them urines).

With whip and chair, Betty forced Albert to trudge around and set a price for each and every urn. I wrote the prices on cards and put each card in a plastic envelope so it could go outdoors on the urns. Even with the huge advertising campaign we were planning, it could take months to sell all the urns. But maybe not. The price was right, and anyone with a pickup truck, King Kong for a helper, and $25 to spend could take home a magnificent example of the urn maker's art.

That was Friday. On Saturday, we sold one of the smallest urns to a gardener who thought it would make a cute birdbath.

Sunday was our day off. We went down to New York to have lunch in celebration of our master plan to "get rid of all those damned urns."

The sun was just starting to set when we returned home. As I turned into the driveway, Betty looked over at the field of urns. She screamed. The field was empty. Every urn was gone, as if whisked away by a giant hand from the heavens.

We raced into the office. Once again, the ledger told the story. A lone entry stared up at us: "Rothbart, 326 urns, $138,000.50."

Albert's original "Price List for Urns" lay beside the ledger. Something about it had changed. A swarm of zeroes had crept into the prices. A wee urn which Albert had decreed worth $1.50 now commanded $250. Medium-sized urns priced at $10 were now $1,000, and big ones capable of holding acres of ivy or the ashes of all our ancestors back to Adam had soared from $25 to $2,500.

Albert explained everything the next day. He was surprised we didn't know the Rothbarts. "Great people!" he said. They have a little place—a couple of hundred acres—down at the shore.

"Well, when Fred called, I had kind of an inspiration. I got on the phone to the Rothbarts' head gardener, Ernie Aquabelasco. It seems the Rothbarts were thinking of replacing all the plastic gnomes and flamingoes they had around the place with something even more elegant. Ernie was very happy to hear from me. He brought up some trucks and carted all the urns away yesterday."

But how come you charged them such fantastic prices?" we asked.

He looked at us pityingly. "You don't know much about rich people, do you? They never buy anything that isn't overpriced. Why, if I had charged them a dollar less, they would think I was unloading a pile of junk on them. I couldn't do that to them. It would destroy their faith in tradespeople."

He never explained the 50 cents on the total in the ledger. But Betty thought it was an admirable touch. Albert, she said, knew how to get the very last drop out of an udder.

Working with plants

Chapter 3

We Shan't Overcome

"How wonderful to be able to work with plants every day!" I shuddered mentally whenever I heard this wistful plaint, and even on my best days I barely managed to summon up a sad smile.

I won't deny that working with plants confers certain benefits to one's health. In those days when "working out" had not yet become fashionable, we worked out with daily marathons and muscle-building regimens worthy of Olympics aspirants. Let me tell you something about the layout of Birst & Borpling Orchids. This paradise for fitness fanatics was situated on about a dozen acres which were entered by a long driveway leading to a pothole-pocked parking area. Albert's home was set a few feet from the road, perfectly placed to allow the headlights of passing cars to illuminate every front and side window at night, The rest of the land sloped up to a wooded area which served as a combination lover's lane and coyote habitat.

About 500 feet back from the road, the office, packing room and potting shed, with our house on top of them, were melded into one building. From this edifice radiated seven greenhouses. Six of them were 200 feet long, the seventh was a little structure nestled into the hillside like an afterthought (which is what it was).

So we had to jog, tramp, shuffle, and on occasion crawl miles in the course of business every day. Sometimes we were burdened only with a pad and pencil for taking inventory or jotting down a description of a new flower for the catalog. More often we were hauling buckets of water filled with cut flowers, or lumbering under the weight of a giant cymbidium in an 18-inch pot.

Occasionally we loped along level ground, but most of the time we were traversing steep inclines or frequent flights of stairs. Three of the greenhouses were fairly level—the main house, so called because the water main feeding it had once burst,

25

floating the plants off the benches; the house, which was partitioned into numerous rooms to accommodate orchids needing different amounts of light, shade or heat; and the very wide out house, so named because it was farthest from the office.

The other three greenhouses rose in tiers on the hillside. These were dubbed the mezzanine, mountain and far-out houses. The seventh was the afterthought I mentioned before, fondly known as the low-down or dungeon house.

When an order came in for a plant in the far reaches of the far-out house, I would quaff a draught of oxygen from my emergency bottle, leap to my feet, and cry, "Up, up and away!" The modern greenhouse has electric carts and conveyor belts. We had only liniment and support hose.

Tickling Trixie

Any greenhouse north of Key West must have a heating system. Ours was a seven-ton mammoth of vaguely menacing aspect. Albert called it Trixie, in honor of his mother-in-law, who shot flaming bolts at him whenever he opened his mouth.

Both Trixies required great dollops of coddling. Our Trixie rumbled away even in summer to supply hot water to our house and to take the chill off the water used on the orchids. But for nine months of the year, it also labored valiantly to produce and circulate hot aqua through pipes under the benches in the greenhouses. Keeping Trixie in good health, we were informed, immediately on arrival at B&B, was our most important job. Let Trixie fail us on just one cold night, and we were out of plants and jobs.

So be it, we thought, and set about learning Trixie's non-negotiable demands. Albert said it was easy. "Not like the old days," he said (he didn't say how old). "Had a coal-fired boiler then. Dad used to call her 'Titanic' until the big ship went down. No icebergs here, but he wasn't one to take chances. Called her 'Teddy Roosevelt' after that, and when the delivery man dumped a load of coal down the chute, he'd holler 'Charge!'"

"When the really cold weather came along, Dad would have two fellows working six hour shifts day and night stoking old

Teddy. That was real work—shovel in some coal, shake the shaker arm, and shovel out the ashes.

"We only had four greenhouses then. The last two big ones were built on the ashes they piled up in back. Somewhere in the attic there is a picture of Dad driving his World War I army surplus truck back and forth across the ashes to pack them down so they could sink the foundations for the mountain and far-out houses."

Old Teddy, he said, was still with us. When Trixie was installed, Teddy was moved over and reconnected to serve as an emergency boiler. Several tons of coal stood ready in a bunker under the office. Albert assured us that we would probably never have to put the old boy back into service. Trixie, like his mother-in-law, never failed to perform as expected, provided she was given the loving attention she knew she deserved.

Albert showed us the three alarm systems that announced Trixie was displeased. One was a factory whistle which warned of insufficient water in the boiler. The second, a clanging bell, told us of a dangerously low fuel supply. Neither of these, thanks to very reliable water and oil suppliers, had ever roused the countryside.

The third alarm signaled a major crisis. Failure to wipe Trixie's eye set off a siren which lifted the roofs off houses down the road.

The eye was an electric eye which detected ignition every time Trixie fired up. If too much soot was allowed to collect on the eye, it couldn't "see" the flame, and it shut everything down and set off the alarm. Restarting Trixie was a tricky process because too much oil had flowed into the ignition chamber without being ignited. He who undertook this task was quickly garbed in thick black soot.

From late spring to early fall, it was only necessary to wipe Trixie's eye every few days. The frequency increased to daily when frosty nights began, and when the temperature dipped to near zero and Trixie worked almost constantly, it was essential to wipe her eye every few hours.

This meant someone had to stay up all night. Betty and I took turns sitting in the office with a pot of coffee, a hook, and a kitchen timer to remind us to run down to the cellar and apply a tissue to Trixie's eye.

Albert came over to relieve us one night when it was eight degrees below zero. Unfortunately, he brought along a bottle of brandy, and the three of us sat around the office imbibing and listening to his endless stories. By dawn, I was bumping on my rump down the narrow cellar stairs and finding it difficult to locate Trixie, let alone her eye. That day Patsy had to take over the eye-wiping job, and the usual twinkle in his own eye dimmed noticeably every time he had to trudge downstairs.

One other operation was mandatory for Trixie's health. Every few weeks in summer and every few days in winter, we had to blow her tubes. This sounds like a gynecological procedure, and indeed it had to do with the proper functioning of her interior anatomy.

It involved starting up an air compressor which was hooked up to one end of the boiler. When a lever was pulled, blasts of air shot through the tubes which carried the burning oil through the water in the boiler. These blasts removed the soot which had built up on the inner walls of the tubes and sent it up the chimney. Blowing Trixie's tubes had to be done at night, and preferably when the wind came from the north so the soot would be blown into the woods to the south. The neighbors were strangely unappreciative of clouds of inky smoke and coats of oily soot on their houses.

Blowing the tubes was a fun job for me. It inspired a special fantasy. Every time I pulled the lever, I envisioned a giant compressor hurling blasts of air to clear traffic jams in all the under-the-river and through-the-mountain tunnels which are commuters' nightmares.

One night when the moon was full, I went outside while Betty worked the compressor. A lovely plume of black smoke was wafting from the top of our 70-foot smokestack. "Ah," I said to myself, "we've made Ringelmann No.4."

What is Ringlemann No.4? Well, Ringelmann is a scale that measure the density of smoke, and No. 4 is at the top of the scale, meaning the smoke is as thick as it can get.

I was satisfied. Trixie would be purring with happiness, for we had unclogged her arteries for at least a few days.

The John from Hell

Once it had been someone's pride and joy. Installed soon after plumbing came indoors, when new, it was one of the finest examples you could find of an inside outhouse. Situated prominently just off the packing room, this restroom extraordinaire had served staff and visitors proudly for nigh on to a century.

Well, perhaps not so proudly in recent times. Its door sagged and could only be closed with a resounding slam, whereupon it would bounce open unless one risked a broken finger or two ramming home the rusty bolt that secured it. When the packing room had been painted a few decades earlier, the outside of the door was included but not its inner surface, nor anything else inside. So this magnificent cubicle appropriately boasted the decor of an orchid jungle, its walls and floor festooned with streamers of black and green mold.

No vestige of porcelain remained on the sink and commode, which were encrusted with a kaleidoscopic bloom of rust like long-submerged marine artifacts. In his weekly cleaning rounds, Gregory refused to do more than open the door just wide enough to hurl in a bucket of hot water and disinfectant.

A special marvel was the wondrous display of pipes. Apparently all the plumbing for the house and greenhouses culminated in this cubbyhole. Gargantuan water and waste pipes ascended, descended and crisscrossed here with all the charm of the boiler room in a battleship. Amazingly, despite their huge promise, these mains delivered more air than water. Flush the john, and you were treated to an eerie sighing sound, followed by thunderous explosions which gradually subsided to a curious jingling like a coin counter in a bank.

Whenever a customer wished to use this facility, we simply pointed to the door, then immediately found pressing business in one of the greenhouse. Unfortunately, I was engaged in shoring up a collapsing packing table and so could not retreat when a certain distinguished visitor expressed a desire to avail himself of our comfort station.

Leaving his suede gloves, walking stick and dove-grey homburg on a table, Count Christabel strode elegantly to the loo. I held my breath, hoping that he was doing the same. After the usual sighing-booming-jingling symphony, the Count emerged, pale under his tan and looking like a tidal wave had washed over him, miraculously leaving his clothing dry. Two steps, and he recovered (blood will tell, I thought). He actually managed a smile, and thanked me for a most interesting and entertaining visit. And as his Rolls pulled out of the driveway, Gregory was in the infamous closet with a magic marker, inscribing "Count Christabel was here" on the wall.

When I told Albert we'd damn well better put in a new comfort facility, he was horrified. "But it would be so…so out of place. It would make everything else look shabby. We'd have to clean up, and fix up, maybe even put in some new light bulbs. My God, what do you want to do, ruin our image?"

Roll Out the Barrels

If the heating system was the heart of Birst & Borpling, water was its lifeblood. Occasional droughts brought restrictions on the use of water by homes and most businesses, but commercial greenhouses were exempted because their very existence depended on the good old H_2O. Although our municipal supply had never failed us, we did try to conserve water; even in those days water cost a little less than wine.

One conservation measure Albert had adopted long ago was a series of several dozen rain barrels lined up on the grass between two of the greenhouses. These collected the runoff from the roofs of the houses quite efficiently, and for years Albert had used a portable pump which he moved from barrel to barrel to feed a hose for watering his wife's roses.

In recent times, though, he had given up this much-too-strenuous task. So the barrels just sat there, filling up nicely when it rained. They weren't exactly quiescent, however. Aquatic life began to appear and proliferate. Since the barrels

Something is breeding in the water barrels!

were ideal breeding places for mosquitoes, the barrels were sprayed frequently with an odoriferous chemical. This pesticide seemed to be the perfect food for some odd organisms. The first to appear was a sort of freshwater jellyfish, a translucent gray blob with yard-long tentacles. These creatures floated on the surface, while up from the depths rose even more repulsive maggot-like critters with long tails. Looking at these, I didn't doubt that if a midget was to don scuba gear and venture into the water, he would see new breeds of muck sharks and bog octopuses reveling in this lovely environment.

The barrels had to go, lest any of the creatures frolicking in them evolve into land dwellers and kill all of us in our beds some night. The easiest way to do this, we agreed, was to knock a hole at the bottom of each barrel and let the water drain into the grass.

Rocco and Gregory did this, while we stood around and cheered each blow of their axes. Problem solved.

Not quite. When the flood abated a few days later, I took a look at the grass. It was a rich green and had grown several inches, as if we had treated it with a miracle fertilizer. But something strange was growing in a few spots. Black globs streaked with bright red and green were sprouting up. I approached cautiously, for they seemed to be pulsing and throbbing.

I yelled for Patsy and the boys to bring some sticks, and we began beating the globs. This was a mistake. Each piece that flew off started to grow and throb on its own. One chunk landed on Patsy's overalls, and he screamed and tore them off.

Albert came out to see what all the hollering was about. At first, he was more concerned by the sight of Patsy jumping up and down in his long underwear. But when he finally understood what was happening, his face blanched and he ran – actually ran– to the office to call a friend who lived across town.

The friend was a retired professor of mycology, a specialist in fungi who looked a little like a shriveled mushroom wearing steel-rimmed glasses. He brought along his kit for identifying fungi, but he needed no equipment to put a name to this baby. He took one look over his spectacles, and shrieked, "My God, it's the Bummermeister fungus!"

He waved us all back, and explained in gasps. "A colleague of mine discovered it last year in Malaya. It was eating plants, dirt, bugs, everything. Terrified old Bummermeister, but he managed to catch and preserve a piece of it in his medicinal schnapps so he could bring a sample home. He used all the spare cans of gas for his Jeep to burn up the rest of it."

He paused to catch his breath. "There's no time to get flamethrowers from the army base. It's only a small patch right now, so we can burn it ourselves. Get some gasoline, rubbing alcohol, booze, anything you can find that will burn – and hurry!" We fell over each other doing his bidding, and in minutes a roaring blaze swept the grass. When it died down, the Professor warned us, "You've got to watch every day for any more of them.

"And for God's sake, burn those barrels. There could be more Bummermeister buggers breeding in them."

"How did they get here?," I asked.

"Who knows? We don't even know how they got to Malaya."

He paused and looked upward, "Some of us think they came from…out there."

When the Professor left, shaking his head and burdened with several bottles of Albert's best bourbon, we set to work. In an hour we had all the barrels piled in the parking lot. Albert called the volunteer fire brigade, and they stood around cheering and manning hoses to wet down any wayward embers. It was the biggest bonfire any of us had ever seen. I knew it was the last one I wanted to see.

The Tenant Upstairs

An attic is great to have for storing things, and the attic at B&B was big. It extended over our house, the office and the packing room, and it housed masses of medals and trophies won by Birst & Borpling orchids over the years, plus box after box of records from the day the business began. And a few million cobwebs and a crust of dust.

We had only gone up to the attic once, when Albert suggested that in our spare time we might construct a display case for the trophies. He also confided that, if he "could only find the time," he would go through all the boxes and write the story of B&B from its beginnings, which would of course be a best-selling multi-volume history of orchid growing in America. The only other visitor to our upstairs museum was Albert's wife, Sylvia, who came over occasionally when in need of a silver bowl to adorn with flowers or fruit for one of her soirees.

We gave the attic very little thought. That is, until one evening after a late dinner, we heard a strange noise over our heads. It was a kind of slithering-rapping-tapping sound, something like a snake gadding about on crutches. We froze, and so did our bulldog. The grimace on Molly's face as she tried to snarl by curling her lips over her undershot jaw gave her the expression of a demented foo dog in a gift shop window. This was almost as frightening as the strange noises overhead. "That's no rat," I whispered. "But nobody could get in. I checked all the doors before we ate."

"He could have broken some glass in one of the greenhouses and sneaked up the back stairs," Betty whispered back. "I bet he's after the trophies. There must be a ton of sterling silver up there."

"You stay by the phone," I said, "I'm going up there."

"Like hell I'm staying here," she snorted. She handed me a cast iron skillet from the stove, and picked up the big lantern we kept for blackouts.

The stairs to the attic were in the packing room. So we tiptoed out there. Our approach was commendably silent, until I happened to bang the skillet against a packing table. The sound reverberated like the gong announcing a J. Arthur Rank movie. Betty dropped the lantern with a crash, Molly began barking hysterically, and the hinges on the door to the attic squealed like a frantic pig when I pulled it open.

Further caution seemed unnecessary, so we charged up the stairs, screaming unintelligible imprecations. There was no one there. Although it wasn't the night before Christmas, not even a mouse was stirring, and we wished we were tucked in our beds.

When Albert came in the next morning, he looked a little peeved.

"Heard you having a party last night. Lots of noise. But there were no cars in the driveway, and you didn't invite me. So I guess it was a private party."

"Party!" I screamed, "Some party. Our guests were giant rats, or bats, or snakes, maybe a whole menagerie in that great attic of yours."

Albert stared, then a huge smile broke out on his face. "So Bicky is back!" he exclaimed.

"Bicky? Who the hell is Bicky?"

"Why, Bicky Birst, of course, Dad's partner. "He has been living in the attic in an old trunk since he died over 50 years ago."

"Oh. come on," I said. "You're telling us we have a ghost? A ghost who loves the place so much he won't leave?"

"Oh, no. Bicky hated the place. He didn't like being cooped up. All he wanted to do was hunt orchids and bring them back alive. He lost a leg doing it. I don't remember if it was snakebite or an infection, but old Bicky ended up with a wooden leg."

He leaned back and lit; his first cigar of the day. "Tap, tap, tap. Bicky was a really energetic cripple, a regular Bojangles of Botany. He died right here, you know, just keeled over in that chair Betty is sitting on. Now the poor fellow just wants to get back to the jungle, but he's trapped in the attic.

"Yes. sir, one of these days I'm going to take that old trunk down to Brazil and leave it in the biggest clump of *Birstia borlingia* I can find. A good idea, don't you think?"

"I think you've got birstia of the brain," I said, and stalked out of the office.

Betty was even less open-minded about the occult than I was. But she took no chances. She brought a broom into our bedroom, and when we heard the tap-tap-tapping again a few nights later, she rapped its handle smartly on the ceiling and covered all bases by bellowing, "Get out, you one-legged, two-legged or four-legged bastard, whoever or whatever you are!"

Attack Of The Killer Philodendron

The attic episode had an odd effect on me. I had never liked working at the lowest end of our establishment, the dungeon house. It wasn't just its cramped size or the heavy shading that made it gloomy. The very high humidity the plants in that house required made the atmosphere dank and dismal.

It was only after the Bicky visitation that I discovered why this house gave me a vague feeling of menace. Just inside its entrance stood a giant philodendron planted many years before by Patsy's Irish predecessor. This venerable philodendron had growth to mammoth proportions, with huge heart-shaped leaves which cascaded down around a network of aerial roots that held it to a hefty tree fern trunk, It was taller than me, and its overlapping drooping leaves made it seem like a disconsolate Peter Pan.

Phil

This green goliath tweaked my subconscious uncomfortably every time I entered the dungeon house. As I sidled past it, the air seemed to become chilly. I began watching Old Phil out of the corner of my eye, and I was certain it moved whenever I turned my back.

Nights were particularly bad. When I had to go down to the dungeon house on a slug-slugging expedition, Phil became the embodiment of some ancient sinister force. In the light of my flashlight, it was Carus, the avenging mummy of the old horror movies. The leaves were the tattered wrappings that held his body together, and I did not dare look up for fear his piercing eyes would transfix me.

Betty was a kindly person, so she stopped laughing in less than five minutes when I told her I felt uncomfortable around Old Phil. Holding her sides, she suggested, "If the big bad green monster scares you, why don't you sell the damned thing?"

A brilliant idea! I had Rocco and Gregory haul Phil up to the packing room, and I set a very reasonable price on him. When there was no buyer in a week, I lowered the price. In another week, I put a sign on Old Phil, "Free – free – free. Take me home – I'm yours."

A couple of days later Phil was gone, departing in a truck driven by a man from a botanical garden who had stopped in to buy some orchid pots. "Magnificent specimen," he said. "Should bring at least $200 at our next plant sale." Little did he know that I was about to offer him that much just to take Old Phil away.

He Peeps By Night

Bicky and Phil were not our only nocturnal nemeses. One evening after supper, we retired to the packing room to make a couple of orchid arrangements which were ordered for the next morning. As usual, I assembled the containers, flower holders and other paraphernalia, then sat down to read my paper until Betty needed me to help pack up the arrangements.

Suddenly I heard a growl from Betty.

"Tom," she whispered, "there's a face at the window."

Very casually, as soon as my heart returned to my chest, I glanced over my paper at the window. She was right. A male visage was pressed against the glass, like a small boy staring wide-eyed at the goodies in a candy store window.

It vanished when I leaped to my feet and raced for the front door. I had been a track star in high school, and despite the four pork chops and three sweet potatoes I had consumed at dinner, I moved fast.

Not fast enough. I saw a short figure already far down the driveway. It moved with the grace of a gorilla but the speed of an ostrich, and it leaped a hedge and was off up the road before I was down our front steps.

By the time I gasped my way back to the packing room, Betty had called the police. A few minutes later, a car with a hundred flashing red lights roared into our driveway. A young Gary Cooper dismounted, complete with Stetson hat, shining boots, and two enormous six-guns at his sides. He trotted up to where we were waiting in the doorway.

"Well, good folks," he drawled, "I hear you have met our friendly Peeping Bob."

"Friendly? Bob?" we inquired in unison.

"Oh, yeah. He's harmless, and his name is Bob. A couple of the gals he's peeped recognized him. They're his patients."

"His patients?"

"Yup. Bob is a shrink. Unfortunately, the gals said they didn't feel like making a positive identification. So the only way we can apprehend this heinous miscreant is if somebody catches him in the act."

Gary hitched up his gun belt and tipped back his Stetson.

"You know, I do believe you folks could help us latch on to this felon. Our records say you keep a gun in your office. Next time you're chasing him, why not put a round into his leg or thereabouts? You'd be saving us a mighty lot of trouble."

I tried to look thoughtful. "Well, now, you know," I drawled, "actually, my wife is a lot better shot than me. A regular Annie Oakley, you might say."

Betty glared at me, but turned her smile back on as she saw a broad grin of approval on Gary's face.

"That's mighty fine," he beamed. "I'll sure look forward to the next time you call me. And I'll bring an ambulance along with my leg irons."

We all shook hands heartily, and Gary mounted his gleaming steed and burned rubber as he exited the driveway. Betty and I sighed and shook our heads. "Of course I could," she mused, "but I don't think I really want to shoot the good doctor if he's harmless."

"Me neither, I said. "And maybe he just wants to learn flower arranging. We should put up a sign – Orchid Arranging Classes, $50 an Hour, Special to Peeping Bobs."

Green Thumbing Our Noses

It annoyed Betty no end, and gave her a persistent tingling in the thumbs of both hands. I'm talking about the landscaping – or rather, the lack of landscaping – on the property known as Birst & Borpling Orchids.

These puny four acres, which had once been meticulously manicured lawns, were populated with dandelions, thistles, hogweeds and who knew what else. The only notable horticultural feature on the place was a lone copper beech which overhung (and periodically invaded) the Borpling home. The giant oaks flanking the entrance to B&B were not the attraction they once had been, one of them having been struck by lightning which seared off three-quarters of its branches.

Betty began modestly. First, she buttonholed Albert's accountant on his quarterly visit. She had no trouble convincing him that putting in a few "really nice" plants would be good for business and also a good investment, since anything that was not a weed was bound to raise the property's value.

Dozens of seed and nursery catalogs came in, scores of orders went out, and hundreds of plants began arriving. All spring, I was left alone every evening to struggle with making corsages while Betty and Patsy (did you ever know an Italian who wasn't one of God's happiest gardeners?) dug, planted, watered and mulched. Dogwoods, flowering cherries, and a hundred raspberry bushes sprang up along the fence on the east boundary. An avenue of trees I had never heard of appeared along the driveway. Patsy appropriated a section in the outhouse to raise countless flats of marigold and zinnia seedlings and geranium cuttings.

The results that first year were colorful if not exactly organized. Albert enjoyed it greatly, and spent many afternoons sitting at the office window with binoculars, exclaiming frequently when a flower opened on a petunia or the leaves unfolded on the ginkgo tree.

Plans were made for many grand new plantings in the fall and next spring. I began to wonder how we would entice customers into the greenhouses when they were greeted by a botanical garden outside. Albert said we could hang some blooming orchids in the branches as soon as the trees grew big enough, and he began planning a lath house just outside the office so even more orchids could be displayed outdoors in warm weather.

Some proposed plantings caused heated arguments. In front of the little porch on the side of our house, there was an ugly box covering the well which had once supplied water to the house and greenhouses. Albert suggested we plant morning glory vines to hide this and decorate the porch, Betty wanted her beloved lilies, and Patsy opted vociferously for his equally beloved giant dahlias.

They compromised. Betty's lilies went into a long bed on the side of the house, which turned out to be the perfect spot for them. Patsy got his dahlias around the well cover, and Albert's morning glories were planted to climb the porch. In front of the old well they decided to grow a plant none of them had ever seen. The castor bean sounded great in the catalog descriptions: a fast-growing tropical shrub with huge leaves and big berries.

When Betty and I returned from a ten-day vacation in July, the offending well cover had disappeared. So had our porch, under a waterfall of morning glories. Betty's lilies obscured our second-story windows. Patsy's dahlias towered and glowered at us in blazing reds and golds. And the castor bean – well, it had shot up to ten feet and its leaves were five feet long.

We all stood around marveling at this jungle. Albert scratched his head and finally came up with the answer to this

Marigolds and morning glories now abound.

40

incredible growth. "You know," he said, "Dad used to keep a couple of cows. There was a barn over there by the fence, and all the manure was piled where your porch is now. That was a good 50 years ago, but this must still be the richest soil in the county. Makes Jack's beanstalk look puny, doesn't it?"

This was not the only time that one of our plantings performed beyond expectations. To mask the massive foundation for the smokestack, Betty chose the silver lace vine. She had read that it was a strong-growing vine with fleecy white flowers. No one told her just how strong-growing it was.

In a few weeks, it had covered the foundation. Then it began creeping up the smokestack. Foot by foot, yard by yard, it rose, its twining stems greedily grasping the bricks. The books say it grows 34 feet long, but apparently this specimen intended to traverse our 70-foot chimney and keep going.

I suggested to Albert that we should fly a big banner with orchids painted on it from the top of this green pillar, or perhaps offer it as a mooring for the Goodyear blimp. He was intrigued by these ideas, but reluctantly vetoed them because the town's zoning laws did not permit signs over six feet above the ground (he didn't know anything about the law on blimps).

Actually, I think he was a little afraid of the vine. Eventually he had it cut down on the advice of his chimney inspector, who said it was sure to bring the chimney down on our heads.

The Melon Man

We made the acquaintance of this inspector of smokestacks one early fall afternoon. A beat-up truck pulled into the parking lot. It was piled high with crates and boxes of vegetables and fruits, and from it alighted a little old man. He stood beside it and appeared to be gazing up into the sky while writing furiously on a pad.

I told Albert, and he exclaimed, "Oh. Lord, it's Iggy. I'd better call the market." He picked up the phone and proceeded to order a crate each of canaries, crenshaws and charantaises. "Iggy loves melons," he explained as he rushed out.

We watched as Iggy and Albert greeted each other with much handshaking and backslapping. After a while, they turned and looked up at our smokestack, which by now was garlanded more than halfway to its summit with the silver lace vine. A flurry of pointing and gesticulating ensued, with tall Albert and short Iggy looking like puppets animated by a crazed puppet master.

This went on for several minutes until the truck from the market arrived and crates of melons were offloaded to Iggy's truck. Iggy departed after another round of even more exuberant handpumping and backthumping, and Albert came back to the office.

He folded himself into his chair and mopped his brow. Our faces showed that no work would get done until he explained the wondrous performance we had just witnessed. "Iggy," he said, "used to work for the state's air pollution control department. They retired him about five years ago, but he just couldn't let go of the job. So he still goes around inspecting chimneys. We see him about this time every year.

"Well, Iggy was always a cooperative kind of guy, and for a box of chocolates or a nice layer cake he'd overlook a minor violation here and there. But since he retired, he has refined his tastes. He built a big root cellar in his backyard, and now he lives well all winter on 'donations' of fruits and vegetables. "

Albert paused to light his ninth afternoon cigar. "Iggy is a nice guy, so we all go along with him. Kind of fussy, though. Loves his melons, but no ordinary cantaloupes for him. It's gourmet all the way. I heard that a grower up the line has to have purple potatoes and ears of pink popcorn shipped in for Iggy.

"By this time next year," he sighed, "we'd better get rid of Miss Silver Lace. Iggy says it will suck out the mortar and make the bricks crumble. But I think the real reason is that it offends him. He sees smokestacks as beautiful things, works of art that should stand there, all clean and bright, through the centuries. He says that man passes, but smokestacks endure.

Our friend, Iggy, I thought, would be right at home in Stonehenge.

Chapter 4

The Customer Is Never Right

There is no place in. the world like an orchid nursery for getting to know human nature. Every day of our sojourn at B&B brought enlightenment through encounters with humblest commoners to royalty both real and self-ordained. Any would-be practitioner of Freud's art would do well to spend a year in training at an orchid emporium.

Don't get me wrong. The majority of our customers were knowledgeable, considerate, and willing to pay a good price for good value. But they were greatly outnumbered in our minds by a few who produced anything from mild twitchings to monstrous migraines.

Among the milder type, I fondly remember a petite lady who badly needed stilts and inch-thick glasses, to whom I showed a plant with long spikes of tiny but exquisitely colored flowers.

"That's nice, dear," she said. "But shouldn't you do something about those awful bugs on its stems?"

Orchid shoppers, we decided early on, could be classified just like orchids. There is the budgeter species who has set a limit of $2 on his purchase. He is interested in pure red or yellow cattleyas, and when told small seedlings of these cost a hundred times his price, he becomes a quivering mass of disappointment. On recovering, he wanders aimlessly around and finally nerves himself to spend $5 on a division of a "common" plant. Actually, he gets a great bargain. By that time, I would have given him the deed to the place to get him to leave.

The wow species has an extremely limited vocabulary. Told the price of a plant, it responds with a resounding "Wow!" accompanied by a sharp blow to the forehead. A less rugged subspecies murmurs its "Wow!" almost reverentially.

The third species always knows exactly what it wants. It walks you briskly through six greenhouses – twice. Halfway through the third trip, it finds itself unable to make a decision and decides to come back later. The trouble is, it always does.

Even more stressful is the orchidolator who prides himself on his knowledge of botanical names. Sometimes I was lucky, as when a gent admiring a batch of cycnoches (sik-noch-ez) asked, "What do you get for these kicknockers?" But when he inquired if we had a kyroptlum, I lost a sale because it took me several excruciating hours to realize the bloke was pining for a cirrhopetalum (which is pronounced just like it looks, except that the "o" is sounded as an "s").

Most apt to provoke biliousness was the know-it-all. One husband-and-wife team admonished me constantly while being shown through greenhouse after greenhouse. He scolded, "You're growing these plants a tad too dry," and she chided, "You are giving them 15 per cent shade when they need 18 per cent." Though molten lava was rumbling in my guts, I forbore remarking that he was wearing a blue shirt with brown pants and she walked like a duck with one leg shorter than the other.

On the other hand, we always strove to aid the true seeker of knowledge. To the question (asked again and again and again), "When do you water your plants", we wrote a rehearsed a stock answer.

"It depends on the kind of plant, its stage of growth, the size of the pot, the potting medium, and of course, the temperature and humidity as well as daily and seasonal variations in the amount of light."

This usually elicited respectful if slightly frustrated looks, followed by, "No, seriously, how often do you water, say, those plants over there?"

I was ready for that one, too. "We water those on the second and fourth Fridays and the first and third Tuesdays of the month. Each plant receives three ounces of water for each inch of diameter of its pot, unless it is growing in osmunda fiber rather than bark, in which case the age and state of decomposition of the medium determines whether it receives two or two-point-five ounces of water per pot diameter inch."

Having once caused apoplexy in a particularly dense inquirer, I was always careful to have a big smile on my face and a twinkle in my eye as I orated this. Light bulbs flashed over the heads of most people, and they responded, "You scamp! You're saying you water the plants when they look like they need it, aren't you?"

"Damn right, buddy. You're going to make a mighty fine orchid grower in a few years."

Conning For Consultants

Get the slightest reputation for expertise in anything, and you become the consultant to consult. An honorable and profitable profession – except in orchids.

Our first consulting assignment was simple. We were asked to appraise a small collection of orchids which its owner was planning to sell so he could replace it with the poppies his fifth wife adored. When we arrived, we found two block-wide greenhouses which seemed to stretch to infinity.

We quaffed a bottle of aspirin, and entered the nearest house to gaze upon row after row of identical plants of identical size. A quick jog down one aisle revealed that every plant was 'Hapless Herkimer', a cattleya hybrid which had been bred before 1900. The view in the second house was the same, except that all the plants in there were an even more ancient hybrid named 'Bunny Buns'.

With gasps of relief, we started counting. Here was a job we could finish in a day. I spoke the first discouraging word when we were enjoying the lunch of green bologna sandwiches (crusts removed) and persimmon juice sent over by the estate's cook. In four hours, we had tallied up something less than five per cent of the plants in one greenhouse.

Obviously higher mathematics was called for. The next day we brought two sophisticated instruments, a tape measure and a hand-cranked adding machine. By counting the number of plants in a row across the eight benches that spanned the width of the greenhouse, then stretching the tape to its full length down along one bench, we were able to calculate the number of plants in a ten-foot length of the greenhouse.

Then it was just a matter of leaping gracefully down an aisle, stretching the tape between us, to determine the number of tape

45

lengths in the house. A dozen or so yards of adding machine tape gave us an incredible but absolutely accurate answer. The following day, after a delightful 60-mile drive in a blizzard, we repeated the job in the other greenhouse.

We were pleased, and naturally we were ecstatic that the venture provided a profit for B&B only slightly less than the minimum hourly wage. Most gratifying of all, we read in the paper a few weeks later that the owner had recouped appraisal cost several times over by selling 201,462 orchid plants for use as landfill for a mall being built on a swamp.

That was our first and last appraisal job. We were tempted, though, by a commission which would have us wafted up to Hong Kong by private jet. Luckily, a friend of Albert's was happy to take on the job. Roger Burlbutt made frequent business trips to the Orient, and he was thrilled, both at the prospect of a free ride and at the opportunity to meet Loretta Luu, the reigning queen of. Hong Kong Society. Rog was eager to appraise her and her orchid collection.

On his return, Rog came out to B&B to tell us all about his fabulous trip. Loretta, he told us, was the favorite illegitimate daughter of the construction mogul who had built most of Hong Kong's skyscrapers. Loretta occupied all four of the penthouses on one of his towering edifices. She had chosen this abode, not for its lavish apartments or spectacular views, but because the terraces encircling the apartments were long and broad. On one of these, she had erected a domed conservatory to house her orchids.

Now this greenhouse and its orchids had to go to make way for Loretta's great dream. She planned to create a rooftop farm that would supply Hong Kong's millions with a cornucopia of succulent comestibles.

Rog took frequent sips of Albert's hundred-year-old brandy as he told his story. "Loretta," he said, gave me all of fourteen minutes to set a value on her orchid palace. Then she pulled me out for a tour of her farm."

He sighed deeply. "There must have been hundreds of huge boxes, tubs and beds. And in them were growing the finest display I have ever seen of parched and stunted corn, tattered squash vines, and nubbins which appeared to be lettuce grown with a blowtorch."

The theme of the farm, he said, was brown, as brown as the overalls worn by Loretta's butler/gardener, a wizened, bespectacled and sake-besotted gnome name Otzo.

Otzo had a no-nonsense approach to farming. "I plant it, then it's on its own." He scorned such frills as watering (which would have required the contents of a small city's reservoir daily), fertilizing (the plants were growing in pure sand), and windbreaks (the breezes on this lofty perch seldom dropped below gale force).

Rog said that although he was a little dazed by the beauty of it all, he managed many bows and murmurs of delight and congratulations on his departure.

He sat back, took another sixty- second sip of brandy, and gave his deepest sigh of the evening. "Loretta's so gorgeous," he said. "I keep picturing her in a diamond tiara and straitjacket."

Unorthodox and Unrepentant

On rare occasions, and only for our very best customers, we visited a home greenhouse to offer a solution to a minor problem its owner was having. Often the problem turned out to non-existent. The owner was really seeking confirmation (in the form of great gushes of adulation) that he or she was doing everything right.

Two of our most spendiferous clients were Kurt and Kitty Lasosa. Retired astrophysicists, they had discovered that no comet or constellation shone as brightly as an orchid.

Every Wednesday afternoon, following their meditation class with the renowned Swami Budhadasa Z. Singasing, Kurt and Kitty arrived at B&B at precisely 3:15 on our sundial, and bought a small truckload of plants. They bought anything with bursting buds, and peeled hundred-dollar bills from wads as thick as longshoremen's fists. When they invited us to lunch, we accepted in anticipation of viewing a truly grand collection.

After a light luncheon of roast pork boulders and mountains of dumplings and sauerkraut, we rolled ourselves out to see the orchids. The greenhouse was a magnificent structure fully eleven feet long and wide, with an odd lean to one side, and basking under giant oak trees.

We entered cautiously, and beheld a rainforest where the rain never ceased. Wall, glass and plants were covered with a green slime that appeared to be alive. Every bulb and leaf sparkled with black rot. Squelching our way across the floor, we dodged collapsing plants and a vine that obviously had man-eating intentions.

Kurt was the chief of the local volunteer fire department, and he had brought his prowess with a hose home to his orchids. He had never read an orchid book, which would have told him that practically all orchids are epiphytes: they live high in trees where breezes quickly dry them off after the torrential but brief tropical rains.

Kurt was also afflicted with a rare form of deafness. A word that even hinted of advice went unheard. Only once did he seem to listen. I suggested that a tiny bit more ventilation might make his orchids grow even better. On their next visit, Kurt reported jubilantly that he had installed two 48-inch fans, one at each end of the greenhouse. "Blow your toupee off!, " he cried.

Not long after that, the Lasosas stopped coming to B&B. We feared that they had been absorbed into the bowels of their greenhouse. Some traveling friends, however, reported that they had visited the happy couple in their new home in Arizona, where they were joyously barbecuing sides of bison and drowning every cactus in the state.

No Crumpets for Me

One morning I took a call from the social secretary of a royal couple who were touring the United States with great fanfare. The Duke and Duchess of Blessmeham, she informed me, grew orchids at their estates at Ugborough near Bittaford, as well as at their villa at Cannes. If it was convenient, they would like to visit our establishment that very afternoon.

My reaction was "royalty-schmoyalty," but Alfred and Betty became dervishes. Albert raced home to shave and change his shirt even though it was only halfway through the week. Betty whirled through the greenhouses with a bushel basket, ripping off a month's supply of cut flowers to strew before each greenhouse (our red carpet was at the cleaners). A staff meeting was called to instruct Patsy and the boys on the proper way to bow and to address the visitors as Your Royal Highnesses.

The tea party

49

The couple arrived in a limousine only slightly shorter than an eighteen-wheeler. As they approached, we all bowed low. They both waved cheerily, and the Duke boomed, "No formalities, please. Aren't we all equals in the world of orchids?"

That was our first surprise. The second was that their highnesses really knew orchids. They harkened graciously as Albert extolled the newest hybrids, but their faces lighted up with child-like joy at certain less flamboyant but really beautiful flowers. Patsy, who was following behind to tag their purchases, beamed as we had never seen him beam before. He and he alone, he insisted, would pack the guests' plants for shipment to England. I heard him growl to Gregory, who was picking up the plants, "Drop that plant, and you die!"

As we left the last greenhouse, the Duchess cried, "Tea time!" She 'signaled one of the footmen standing at attention beside the limousine and he quick-marched up the walk bearing two huge picnic baskets. A lace tablecloth was spread on the biggest table in the packing room. The Duke himself brewed the tea on our hot plate, and the Duchess laid the table. With silver tongs that weighed a few ounces but must have cost a few hundred pounds, she spread an array of tea cakes which would have shamed the dessert cart at a ten-star restaurant.

While we were dining perched on the high stools we used while making corsages, the Duke entertained us with tales of their travels. Our favorite described a trek in Africa where they were accompanied by the Minister of Zisyphus Development. For his work in having bore holes dug to bring water to their crops, the tribe presented the Minister with a life-sized wood carving of his likeness attired in a leopard skin and carrying a great spear. The Duchess received a coverlet made of the skins of hyenas.

The Duke was given the finest gift all. With great blowing of rhinoceros horns, the chief of the Zizyphus tribe presented him with a little girl about five years old. To refuse such a gift would have been awfully bad manners, so the Duke had to think fast. With great regret, he informed the throng that in his country only the king was permitted to have more than six wives. Since he already had his full allowance, he asked that the child be

The minister.

installed in a place of honor in the household of the chief himself (who happened to be 97 years old). For this magnificently generous gesture, he was acclaimed with stupendous cheers, led by the Duchess.

When the royal couple departed our establishment, the Duke raised his hand in the Churchillian "V" sign, and the Duchess blew kisses at us. Only one thing had marred their visit. Of the dozens of crumpets the chefs at Blessmeham had baked for their trip to Colonies, only two were left for our tea. Albert was given one, Betty the other. I watched, holding back tears, as Albert consumed his with ostentatious relish.

Betty, however, very carefully wrapped hers in a doily and announced that it would be the crowning glory of her bedtime snack. The next day she had it bronzed, and today it still resides in a glass cabinet I had had made to display the trophy we had won for growing orchids on the windowsill of a Second Avenue tenement.

We Are Shown the Future

I have often wondered how their Highnesses would have reacted to a certain gentleman from Holland. Probably with their usual graciousness, although certain of their ancestors had been known to draw and quarter such persons.

Gustave Boskoom turned up at Birst & Borpling early one morning and walked through the greenhouses with an oversized pad on which he made copious notes. But I noticed something odd. He never looked at the plants. With each step, his eyes swept from floor to roof, as if he expected to be swallowed up in a massive cave-in or buried under an avalanche of glass. Sometimes he kneeled and peered under the benches, then rose to bend over backwards and stare at the peak of the greenhouse.

I told Albert about this, and he blanched. This was something he had always dreaded. The fellow was undoubtedly an inspector sent by some government agency. The greenhouses his grandfather had built were about to be condemned as unsafe for human or orchid habitation. The doors would be sealed and giant signs posted to inform the world that he had been endangering the public by maintaining hazards too horrendous to contemplate.

By the time Herr Boskoom came to the office, Albert was in a state of near-collapse. His conditioned worsened when Boskoom announced solemnly, "Lady and gentlemens, I have important news for you."

Settling his ample bulk in a chair, he proceeded to explain. In his country, which was the world leader in production of flowers and where greenhouses covered more acres than cities, there was a labor shortage. He and he alone had solved this problem. He had invented the "autorchouse."

This fully automated facility for growing orchids would enable a single (or even married) person to operate a million square feet of greenhouses without stirring from his chair. The Boskoom automated orchid house was framed in stainless steel that never needed cleaning. Colored fluids circulated through triple layers of plastic glazing to provide the ideal degree of shading moment by moment as the sun moved across the sky. Microscopic sensors implanted in the roots of the plants constantly monitored their use of water and fertilizer, and supplied everything needed in parts-per-million instantaneously.

His engineers, Boskoom said, were perfecting robots that could divide and repot thousands of plants per hour. It was only a matter of time until they developed robotic systems to cut and pack the flowers. And the control panel for all this wizardry, he stated, would be no larger than the one NASA used at Houston for trips to the moon.

All this, he said, could be ours for the paltry sum of 3. 5 million dollars (plus cost overruns).

Albert had not said a word during this presentation. Now he tottered to his feet. Uttering a piteous moan, he staggered out and ran towards his home. Betty and I ushered a perplexed Herr Boskoom to his car, valiantly resisting impulses to administer a few kicks to speed him on his way.

Albert's wife, Sylvia, came over later to machete us for upsetting her dear little man. We barricaded ourselves in the office and held up a sign saying, "Not our fault – Albert assaulted by an idea that would cost money."

This apparently was an adequate explanation. She left, and we retired to a soothing repast of tea, toast and Pepto Bismol. And in less than a month, Albert left his bed and returned to help restore B&B to its normal state of placid chaos.

The Case of the Purloined Pollen

Today security devices once known only to James Bond are commonplace. The smallest bank or bodega can foil the malefactor with howling alarms, steel shutters that hurtle down to seal every exit, and jets of sleepy-time gas.

Back in the days of our orchid odyssey, our only weapon was eternal vigilance. Our forefathers saw this as the price of freedom; we knew it to be the price of freedom, from the poorhouse. Certain orchid lovers made frequent pilgrimages to Birst & Borpling for the sole purpose of relieving it of its treasures. Added up, their depredations were as devastating as wee-hour visits by crews of burglars with moving vans.

Some thieves we almost hated to foil, such as the little man we called the Scavenger. After wandering through the greenhouses and buying one very inexpensive plant, he would walk around outside to admire the landscape. Especially worthy of his admiration was the compost heap where Patsy threw backbulbs, the little not-worth-potting pieces left over when dividing plants. He stuffed his pockets with these, and a few years later-was winning awards for our discards. His scavenging came to a grinding halt when we bought an old shredder at a yard sale, which Patsy used gleefully to convert backbulbs into mulch for his cucumbers.

One blue-haired gentlewoman who arrived in a maroon Bentley always carried an umbrella which she kept closed but loose. As she toured a greenhouse, she would bend rapturously over a plant, her fingers wielding a little custom-made hybrid of toenail clippers and pruning shears. A quick snip, and a nice little division of the plant vanished into the umbrella.

Albert never dared to confront this doyenne of filchery; he sat staring out the window at the Bentley all the time she was there. But one day as she was leaving, I accidentally tripped and managed to up-end her bumbershoot. When I pulled out my pad and pencil to tally up her 'purchases," she became indignant. "But you have so much, and I have so little!"

Another Raffles even I never ventured to bring to justice called herself Granny Annie. She drove a former armored car, and her huge frame was encased in a voluminous greatcoat in July as in December. Granny Annie only liked big plants, and she acquired sizable portions of many a giant cymbidium and dendrobium. Down from the sleeve of her coat would slide toppers, those overgrown shears tree surgeons use to slice off branches as thick as their arms. "Snap" went the toppers, and a chunk of orchid plant found a new home in Granny's greatcoat.

We rationalized our reluctance to apprehend Granny Annie by observing that (a) she pillaged us only a couple of times a year, and (b), she was not blessed with good taste in orchids and confined her hacking to plants with flowers too miserable even to send down to our cut-flower wholesaler.

Granny Annie was the most formidable of our adversaries, but the doctor who suffered from hay fever was the most crafty. Dr. Bobbins was a hybridizer of orchids, a famous one. Like Albert, he had an unerring instinct for breeding an exceptionally beautiful orchid with another great beauty to create one that made its parents look shabby.

To make his crosses, Dr. Bobbins needed pollen. Wherever he went, he carried a supply of those little zip-up plastic bags. Spying a flower that was just right for crossing with one his plants, he bent over it and held an open bag next to the flower. He gave a violent sneeze that propelled every grain of pollen into the bag, which then disappeared into a big handkerchief with which he blew his nose.

Dr. Bobbins' forays were especially vexing to Albert. All too often, Albert had made the same cross, only to find the Bobbins hybrid blooming, winning awards and being marketed lucratively before his had popped its first bud. The ingenious doctor, it seems, had invented a method of speeding up the growth of his seedlings with blazing lights and torrents of fertilizer and water so that they shot up like tots fed a super vitamin.

This had to stop, before Albert speeded up his own rate of nervous breakdowns. Scotland Yard, we heard, has a special unit to investigate plant thefts. Having no such resource, we had to come up with deterrents of our own. On a trip to the city, I stopped in a store that sold burglar alarms, and bought one that blended siren howls with klaxon horns capable of summoning sailors to battle stations on an aircraft carrier.

We worked out a simple drill. When a known purloiner visited, I waited two minutes and twenty seconds, then sidled into the greenhouse behind the miscreant. One minute and thirty seconds later, Betty triggered the alarm system. Smiling cheerily at the suspect, I said, "Oh, that's nothing. Just someone trying to steal a plant. Don't worry, the dogs will take care of him."

The perpetrator either became a non-perp or never darkened our door or balance sheet again. It worked so well that we were tempted to use it whenever a busload of avid aquisitors descended on us, but our insurance agent informed us that he could not cover injuries incurred in stampedes.

Little Girls Think Big

One customer whom Albert treated with deference bordering on reverence was Amelia Kahtz-Piser. Amelia grew orchids on a glassed-in terrace on a high-rise overlooking Boston's Charles River. Every few months for many years, Albert had been sending Amelia a selection of the best plants he had in bloom.

Then disaster struck. Amelia's husband Oscar vanished, along with several million dollars belonging to the gypsum company he headed. Amelia was devastated. She would have to move to a smaller, terrace-less apartment and give up her orchids. Albert immediately dispatched us to convey his condolences, and incidentally to let Amelia know that he was willing to buy back her orchids, naturally at a reduced price since they would need skilled and laborious repotting and rehabilitation.

Amelia was not what we expected. A tiny woman with a magnificent mane piled like a platinum spire on her head, she was plain of face but had eyes of steel. She looked me up and down, then she noticed Betty. "Oh, you brought your wife," she said. I thought I detected a trace of disappointment underlying the cordiality in her voice, but of course I was imagining things.

Amelia wasted no time on chit-chat. She accepted our (or at least my) expressions of sympathy with a deep shrug and a slight inclination of her head (anything more than slight and her pillar of hair would have tipped her over). Serving us instant coffee and barely warmed pigs-in-blankets from a microwave standing alone on a forty-foot-long sideboard, she draped herself over a fuchsia-and-gold chaise lounge.

"Of course, I want dear Albert to have my orchids. The sweet things have grown quite a bit, so he can chop them up and make three or four plants from each one. I think a fair price would be…" She-quoted a sum equal to B&B's gross for the next decade.

Leaving us no time to recover, she went on. "Dear Mr. Bowell, Albert has informed me that you are acquainted with numerous persons in the horticultural field. According to a beautiful young Viking from the FBI, even if they find that bastard and Oscar's stash, I am not likely to receive any more income from his firm. Therefore" – she paused to dab her eyes with a lace handkerchief worth at least a month of my salary – "I will be compelled to seek WORK."

Suitable employment, she said, would utilize her talents to direct the fortunes of a major horticultural enterprise. With her at the helm, it was inevitable that said company would rapidly soar to the single-digit ranks of the Fortune 500.

My mission was simple. Mr. Bowell was to arrange for the chief executives of appropriate firms to meet with her and be shown how she planned their meteoric rise to the ionosphere of profit. As a special concession, she was willing to meet them in New York, provided, of course, that they would defray the expense of her first-class flight and suite at the Plaza. And for his services in introducing them to this great asset, Mr. Bowell would undoubtedly receive a handsome finder's fee.

Awed by the magnificence of Amelia's vision, we were speechless. Out of the corner, of my eye, I saw that Betty's face was taking on that peculiar shade of mauve that meant she was about to start exhaling brimstone. Expressing our great eagerness to get started on this privileged mission, we left precipitately, with Amelia waving us on with uplifted diamond-encrusted fists.

Albert was dozing in the office when we got back home. We hated to disturb his dream, so we waited two seconds before informing him of Amelia's terms for repossessing his orchids. His reaction was surprising.

"Ah, she hasn't changed a bit. How marvelous!

"In my softest and most diplomatic tones, I screamed, "What the hell are you talking about?"

He sat back and repositioned his feet on his desk. "Nothing to worry about. In a couple of weeks, I'll call her and ask how she's doing. By that time, she'll have found a new man who is able to support her in the style to which she insists on being accustomed. She'll be ready to order some more orchids."

"And what about this job she wants us to get for her?"

"Oh, that, too, shall pass. In fact, it probably passed about six minutes after you left. You see, Amelia has very imaginative fantasies. She sees herself as ruling a world populated only by herself and a few million adoring men."

He leaned back and stared at a Rorschach water stain on the ceiling. "Once, a very long time ago, I almost asked Amelia to marry me. She could sell orchids to the trees they were growing on. When I think of what she could have done for this place..."

"So you sent us all the way to Boston for nothing?"

"Oh, no. I couldn't deny you the pleasure of meeting Amelia, could I? Now you can tell everyone you have seen the greatest of all hybrids, Pygmy crossed with Amazon."

We had to admit he was right.

Chapter 5

Hybes, Pews and Wuckles

Every orchid business has multiple personalities, and anyone who grows orchids for a living must wear many hats, not all of them either fetching or comfortable.

The main source of income for Birst & Borpling was the sale of plants to orchid hobbyists, but cut flowers were also an important bread-and-butter commodity. Practically all our cattleyas, cymbidiums and cypripediums were grown for their flowers, which were sent to a local wholesaler who peddled them on commission to area florists.

Twice a week we packed and graded our cuts. All cattleya flowers had to be separated by types – colored hybrids, whites, and whites with colored lips. We called them hybes, pews and wuckles. Some florists demanded only hybes, others bought only pews and wuckles.

When the boxes were packed, we trundled them in our station wagon down the road to the establishment known as Sal's Wholesale Flowers. All this was an easy routine, except at certain high-demand holidays, or when the wholesaler called frantically for a hundred spikes of cymbidiums for the annual banquet of the plumbers and steamfitters union. In the latter case, our usual casual assembly line looked like Lucy and Ethel packing chocolates at the candy factory (if you remember that famous episode of "I Love Lucy," you're old enough to be reading this).

Sal of Sal's Wholesale had handled Albert's flowers for many years. Al and Sal had a mutually wary and grudging respect for each other. Not exactly buddy-buddy, but Sal knew he could count on Al to supply him with fairly decent flowers, and Al trusted Sal to get fairly decent prices for most of the stuff he sent.

Every so often we got a call from another wholesaler a few towns away. Tony supplied only mortuaries. He bought cattleyas by the hundreds for casket blankets. Apparently these were ordered by clients who used them for the funerals of colleagues whose departures they had been compelled to arrange in the course of their businesses.

Tony preferred to be called Tone, and he had a silky smooth voice. His conversations on the phone never varied. "I need you honeys to get together ten or twelve dozen cats, big whites with purple lips. Make sure they're nice ones, nice nice ones. No dogs. I can't afford to have barkers in my blankets, ha ha."

After the first few calls, my conversation became as unvaried as his. "Sure thing, Tone. Only the toniest flowers for Tone, ha ha."

Tone got his nice nice ones, and we were paid promptly and well. Which goes to show, I guess, that it pays to deal with certain organized elements of society. They, too, love flowers, for special occasions, and nothing says love like a big bunch of wuckles.

Unkind Cuts

Old habits die hard, and sometimes they need quick and merciful killing. Something like a hundred years ago, a certain cattleya hybrid had been the darling of the cut flower trade. Florists considered 'Passion Purple' the perfect corsage orchid for the Rubenesque Victorian maiden.

'Passion Purple' was big, really big, with purest white petals and luscious red-purple lips. It had just one fault. It was strictly a one night-stand flower. Within 24 hours of being cut, it flopped, going limp like a cobra chomped by a mongoose. Betty called it a B-29 put together with toilet paper rivets.

But Albert loved them, perhaps because his wife and five daughters all tended to Rubenesque proportions. He had at least a thousand plants of 'Passion Purple' taking up a large section of a greenhouse. When they flowered, he bustled into the office and announced that all hands would be cutting "the ladies" to get them down to Sal that very day.

Betty and I were still toiling long after everyone else went home for the night. I cut the flowers and brought them in, and Betty put each stem in a tube of water and carefully nestled the bloom in shredded waxed paper in a box. The next morning I took two station wagon loads down to Sal's and piled the boxes as usual by the doors of his refrigerator rooms.

When we went down later that week with other flowers, there the boxes were, right where we had left them. Sal came out, looking unhappy.

"Look," he said, "every year I tell Al the same thing. I can't waste space in my coolers for crap nobody will buy. Well, I don't say nothing to him no more. I'm telling you. You got a compost heap. Put those damn flowers on it."

We lugged all the boxes home and did just what he said. Albert was watching as I tossed wheelbarrow loads of "Passion Purple' flowers on the compost heap. He kept shaking his head and muttering, "I don't understand. I just don't understand." Neither he nor we mentioned his "ladies" again, but it was obvious to us that we would have to do something if we did not want to go through the same thing all over again next year.

"We've got to sell the plants," Betty said. "Sell them?," I said. "I'll pay people to take them away." And that's what I did. From that day on, every visitor was presented with two crisp dollar bills and a plant of the "historic Victorian orchid," whether he wanted it or not.

When the last plant of 'Passion Purple' went out the door, Patsy was ecstatic. It meant no more annual repotting of "those useless anticks." And Albert – well, several times we spied him carrying trays of seedlings into the space vacated by his departed ladies. He let it be known that he had had the brilliant idea of disposing of all those old cats to make way for the new hybrids which were going to make us all rich.

To Ship or Not To Ship

One day while rooting around in some battered old files in the office, I came across a batch of invoices from a wholesaler in New York City. Even though they were dated many years ago, the prices we were paid for our flowers then were quite a bit higher than were currently getting from Sal.

The destruction of Albert's flowers

I mentioned this to Betty, and with our usual lightning flashes of inspiration, we came up with an idea a month or so later. Why not send some flowers down to the big city?

I called the Big Apple wholesaler the next day. When I told him we were working at B&B, he said, "Geez, it's been twenty years since I heard from that place. What the heck are you doing there?"

"Right now we're resurrecting the cut flower business here. We can send you some really good orchids if you are interested. "There was a pause. "Only if they won't be the lousy stuff your place used to send me," he grunted.

"I sure don't need any washed-out cats and dirty cymbidiums."

"Oh, you won't get any of those," I promised.

"Suppose I send you a trial shipment?"

We finally agreed, and he told me that the freight company he used still had a key to our front door. All we had to do was leave the boxes of flowers just inside the door, and the driver would pick them up around three in the morning after we called. I consulted Betty on what we could send. She thought about it for several moments, then had a vision (I called them hallucinations, but sometimes...). Never mind the cattleyas and other common florist's orchids. Her inner eye saw all the great sprays of dancing ladies, the gorgeous lady's, slippers, Hawaiian dendrobiums, brilliant vandas and vuylstekearas whose flowers always went to waste unless someone bought the plants.

As soon as Albert went home that afternoon, we began a treasure hunt. We scoured every greenhouse, harvesting blooms in bottles and buckets. Supper was forgotten as we packed and addressed the boxes. A call to the freight company, and the die was cast.

"Not a word to Albert," we kept saying to each other. We knew he wasn't likely to catch on, since there were still many plants we hadn't denuded of flowers, and anyway, the only greenhouse he visited with any regularity was the seedling house, where he would stare for hours at tiny plants as if willing them to bloom. This venture was one of those secrets which, if it didn't pan out, would be quietly buried in the compost heaps of our minds.

A few days later, an envelope arrived from the wholesaler. Betty looked over my shoulder as I opened it, and we both gaped at the check. The amount on it was several times the monthly sum we averaged from Sal's Wholesale Flowers.

Without a word, I handed the check to Albert. He looked at it, then looked at us, and looked back at the check. He shifted around on his hemorrhoid ring and finally asked, "What is this?"

Betty handed him the list of flowers we had sent to New York. "Just a few things we thought a Park Avenue florist or two might find a use for."

Albert stared at the check again. "Hmmm," he said. "Hmmm, hmmm, hmmm," He got up and walked out.

All that afternoon he prowled around the greenhouses. When he returned to the office, he sat down, breathing heavily from his exertions.

"Children," he said, "we have a lot of unusual flowers. I was thinking that some of the fancy florists in New York might really appreciate them. Maybe we should try a few shipments into the city. It might just be profitable."

It was our turn to breathe heavily. All we could do was look at him in awe and say, "Where did you ever get such a great idea?"

Albert just smiled. He knew where, but he sure as hell was not going to say it.

Just Make The Arrangements!

Betty had never made a flower arrangement before coming to B&B. So panic was the order of the day when a certain Mrs. Birdee called to order the usual arrangement for her anniversary party.

An emergency call to Albert brought a surprising response. Here was something he liked to do. "Birdee," he said, rubbing his hands together, "wants it big and colorful, a knockout centerpiece that overflows the table. Well, let's give it to her."

He herded us up to the attic, and opened a cobwebbed cabinet to reveal a cache of containers of every size and shape. He blew the dust off the biggest one, a wide blue porcelain bowl which was cracked but could still hold water.

"Downstairs," he commanded. "Wash this, and get all the flower tubes, stem holders, foam and clay you can find. I'll pick some posies."

All was ready when he returned with a bucket of posies that included tall spikes, arching sprays, and a generous helping of huge single flowers, plus a basket of cut ivy.

"Now let's see what you can do with this," he said to Betty. I stepped back hurriedly, expecting at least some minor hysterics. But Betty set her jaw and narrowed her eyes, and fingers began flying. Stems were stuck in tubes, needle holders, and blocks of foam or clay, and flowers began sprouting all over the bowl. Each flower was popped and propped into place without hesitation, as if she had done it a thousand times before. Finally ivy was woven in among the flower stems and cascaded over the edges of the bowl.

The result was, to use a current expression, awesome. Given all the different flower shapes and polyglot colors, it would have been a garish mess, but it was beautiful when viewed from any angle. Albert looked startled, but managed a grudging nod of approval. The best he could do was move a spike a centimeter to one side or push a stem a millimeter deeper in its holder.

Betty wasn't one to waste time collecting accolades. She asked Albert, "What do you usually charge for something like this?"

"Oh, I think $25 is about right," he said.

Betty yelped. "That's ridiculous. You don't get orchids and artistry for peanuts, buster. A hundred dollars and not a cent less, or I quit."

Albert clutched the edges of the table. "Mrs. Birdee will never pay that," he mumbled.

"Oh, no? Let me give it to her when she comes, and I'll teach her something about the value of good flowers and good work."

Albert had no answer to this. He held his head in his hands and went home.

When Mrs. Birdee arrived, a tiny woman in a mammoth station wagon driven by a Greek god chauffeur, she was treated to a resounding dissertation on everything from the value of an odontoglossum flower to the plight of the underpaid floral artiste. Betty talked for a full ten minutes, during which Mrs. Birdee fluttered her hands continuously as if preparing to take flight. At the end, the Birdee smiled – really grinned –and wrote out a check, and then summoned her chauffeur to bear the treasure to the car. Albert, peeking out of the office window, saw them prancing in a kind of triumphal procession to their chariot.

From then on, Betty ruled the arrangements roost. Although she never admitted it to me, I think, she was a little surprised that she could create floral extravaganzas that would be the envy of a Sorbonne-trained artist. She didn't seem surprised, though, that she could persuade the cheapest harpie to part with what they were worth.

One incident reduced Albert to gibbering. Mrs. Humbleton was famous for her very particular tastes, and for taking no sass from tradespeople. She always demanded certain orchids for her birthday bash, and they had to be arranged in a certain Oriental style to complement her decor.

Unfortunately, none of the plants Mrs. H. insisted upon was blooming at the crucial time. Albert wanted to call every orchid grower in his address book to find them, but Betty made an arrangement with the flowers she had on hand. Even Albert had to admit that it was one of her best creations, but he predicted the loss of a valued customer, and he suffered an attack of pitiful palpitations when Betty priced it at five times the $15 which was the most Mrs. H. ever spent.

The day after the Humbleton birthday, Albert happened to answer the phone when Lady H. called. We saw him flinch, and he seemed to be unable to say anything but hello. Finally he muttered, "Thank you so much," and hung up.

He reached for his inhaler and sniffed and whiffed until he was able to breathe again. Then he croaked, "Mrs. Humbleton says her g-g-guests thought the arrangement was the m-m-most beautiful thing they had ever seen. She wants more for all her d-d-dinner parties."

He never again questioned Betty's handling of a customer.
We had lots to learn, but so did he.

Pin It on the Horse

A florist's business, at least in those days, depended largely
on corsages. And as I've said before, the cattleya orchid was the
traditional corsage flower, an essential accessory for the female
shoulder, waist or wrist at every prom and wedding.

Not wanting to be in competition with the local florists, we
generally left corsage making to them. There were two
exceptions. One was a one-time thing we never repeated, the
other shook our confidence to the core.

The first was a request, relayed pleadingly to us by Albert
from one of his daughters. She wanted us to provide corsages, at
cost, for all the members of her class for their senior prom. We
spent a day and most of a night using every cattleya flower, roll
of ribbon and corsage box we had, putting together 143 corsages.
The reward for our labor was a magnificent 75 cents per corsage,
which the class treasurer paid only eight months later.

When the same request came in from the junior prom, Betty
suddenly came down with a combination of arthritis, carpal
tunnel syndrome, and a nervous tic that gargoyled her face.

That ended our corsage endeavors, except for the annual
equine extravaganza held at Madison Square Garden. The Horse
Show afforded the supreme opportunity for every female in the
saddle to flaunt her most flamboyant finery at the ball after the
show. Said finery, of course, had to be embellished with the
most splendiferous flowers. Since B&B resided in horse country
where stables outnumbered garages, we were the traditional
source of blooms for the well-endowed woman who rode.

They began calling in their orders weeks before the show.
Years earlier, Albert had started keeping a file of each lady's
preference in flowers. We figured that these were based on
physical characteristics – big flowers for the huge gal, small for
the petite, etc.

We were wrong. The horsy set has its own rules. The littlest ladies favored blimpy blooms with scads of ribbons, those of overabundant avoirdupois were happy only with tiny flowers in micro-mini bouquets with just a smidgen of ribbon. "Peanuts on watermelons, watermelons on peanuts," was how Betty described it.

I was totally confused. Although each box was tagged with the customer's name I was never sure that I was giving the right corsage to the right person.

For weeks after the show, we tended to see people and flowers as either bigger or smaller than they really were. A kind of fun house mirror distortion kicked in every time a customer came in for a corsage. And Albert seemed to think that Betty's response whenever a corsage was ordered was a little peculiar.

She would cry, "To horse, to horse!" and gallop off to the packing room, whinnying and retching all the way.

Corsage customers

Chapter 6

Stocking Up

Albert ordered supplies only when need became crisis. Patsy had learned long ago to roar at him, "We gotta get more bark!" while keeping several dozen bags in caches under various greenhouse benches.

Back then, we didn't have computers to keep track of inventory. Dearths and shortfalls were the order of the day. On our very first week on the job, we could not do the payroll because Albert had not remembered to order new checks when the checkbook ran out. That same week, we cut hundreds of flowers to send to Sal's Wholesale, only to find we had no boxes to pack them in.

Patsy kept Rocco and Gregory busy scrubbing algae-coated clay pots so they could be used again, and he threatened them with deportation to the bowels of the earth is they should ever break a pot. But there was always a famine in the potting shed, with relief aid constantly needed in the form of round pots, square pots and squat pots in one size or another.

We once asked Patsy why he did not use the mountains of plastic pots that adorned the back yard of our house.

"Rotten roots!" he bellowed. When the purple had left his face, he explained. These (many expletives deleted) things did not "breathe." They did not exhale moisture like the pores of clay pots, and his precious roots stayed wet too long.

"The big boy should know better," he snarled. It was the only time we ever heard him criticize his boss. Albert had done the unforgivable. He had bought a hundred gross of these pots when they first came on the market, not because they were lighter and almost unbreakable, but simply because they were cheaper. Patsy had been left to hurl them out the door screaming, "Rotten roots! Rotten roots!"

We solved the supplies problem by primitive means. Stone tablets being hard to find, we made up a giant ledger, with pages for each major item and sub-pages for minor ones, plus sub-sub-pages for items like corsage ribbons which had to be classified by size, color and composition. When the ledger became too thick and heavy to handle, we made up another and then another. The use of every nugget of bark and inch of ribbon was recorded.

Albert marveled at this feat, and we were satisfied, even though our backs became permanently bowed from poring over the ledgers like Cratchets keeping the books for Scrooges.

"We Got Foin"

Growers had recently started potting their orchids in a mix of bark, peat and perlite. This was nice and fluffy and easy to stuff into pots, and the orchid roots got plenty of air. But it only stayed that way for a matter of months. The bark and peat broke down and became soggy, necessitating annual repotting in fresh mix.

Much longer lasting, the old-timers knew, was fern. The wiry black roots of the native osmunda fern which grew in swamps was the ideal potting medium for orchids. It had fallen out of favor only because it caused the deformity known as osmunda arm (from which Patsy, as I mentioned before, suffered in the extreme).

Patsy, however, swore by osmunda fern, and Albert had a secret source. We learned the secret one morning when we were jolted out of our chairs by thunderous backfires emanating from a truck of 1920s vintage chugging into the driveway.

"Ah, another eccentric millionaire," I thought. This notion was not dispelled by the couple who alighted from the truck, but I revised it to "millionaire hippies trying to look like hillbillies," and wondered if the truck was loaded with casks of cornsqueezin's.

Our visitors stuck unsmiling faces unto the office, accompanied by a strange and strong odor. They uttered just three words: "You want foin?"

Albert unfolded himself from his chair. "Well, now," he said. "It sure seems like I do want fern. Why don't you all just show my boys how to unload your truck, and I'll go root around in my stash of cash."

He ushered them out, and we rushed to open the windows. When he returned, he answered our unspoken question.

"That's Ned and Nellie. They live in the swamp. If you ever need any cohosh root or copperhead venom, they're the people to see. They've been cutting fern as a favor to me for nigh on to twenty years. Seem to think I'm some sort of kinfolk."

"How come you forgot to ask after Cousin Zeke and Grandma Hepatitis?," I asked.

"Well, snap my suspenders, so I did. Oh, well, Ned and Nellie will be back again around pumpkin stealin' time."

He stood up. "Guess I'd better mosey on out and tell Uncle Patsy he's got some foin to play with. Got to beat the crap out of it, you know."

The beating of the foin, he explained, was necessary to get the dirt, bugs and snakes out of it. Great clouds of dust rose as Patsy, Rocco and Gregory wielded baseball bats with gusto and much uttering of battle cries in their native tongues.

"Good therapy," Betty commented. "I guess we can stop worrying about Uncle Patsy and his boys hacking us to death in our beds tonight."

The Tree Fern Follies

There was another fern, coveted by every orchid grower but seen by few. A tall tree-like tropical plant, the Mexican tree fern had aerial roots that were almost impervious to rot. Their fibrous strands lasted for years, even for the grower who had a heavy hand on the hose. But this wonder material was rare in the wild and even rarer in commerce.

And thereby hangs a horrendous tale.

One of Albert's favorite pen pals was a venerable professor of botany at the university in Mexico City. Albert and Steve Balmbucher had met just once nearly four decades ago, but they had been buddies by mail ever since. They traded orchid gossip back and forth across the border with the verve of washwomen hanging over the back fence.

One day a letter came from Steve that made Albert take his feet off his desk. Steve had discovered the mother lode, a source of Mexican tree fern in great quantities fresh from the fens. His nameless supplier was ready to out and ship by the carload, and the price was right.

Here was THE BIG DEAL. Albert could corner the Mexican tree fern market. Orchid growers everywhere would hail him as a hero as they hurled greenbacks at him for bales and slabs of the precious stuff. Albert bit through his cigar and chortled. "We can build a shed a hundred feet long back of the outhouse, and we'll get some saws and wood chippers to process the stuff. We'll advertise in every orchid magazine. We'll need more phones to take the orders, and we had better alert our shipping company to put on more trucks."

"Whose," I said. "I see in Steve's letter that he needs a bank draft that's more than five times what he is paying for the fern, to cover shipping costs."

"Oh, that's nothing," Albert waved it away. "There is a permit or two you have to get before sending anything out of the country. Steve has to work through a broker, and the officials who issue the permits need, er, some little inducements to keep the ball rolling."

"You mean bribes," I asked.

"Well, let's think of them as contributions to these hard-working fellas who will keep our fern zipping along."

Contributions to fat bellies and fatter haciendas, I thought. But Albert knew what he knew, so off went the bank draft.

A month later, a cable from Steve informed us, "Freight cars of fern on siding 100 miles from dock. Send funds for special rolling permits."

We sent him more money, and each week more funds went south for more rolling permits. Sidings apparently abounded along the rail line, and at each one, freight had to be inspected and a permit issued.

A couple of months later, Steve cabled to say that his broker, known only as Raoul, had reported jubilantly that the fern was on the dock. Only one minor detail prevented its being loaded on the ship. The Customs force at the port had recently been doubled, and of course it was necessary to encourage these officials to expedite the processing of the hundreds of documents that now accompanied our shipment. Raoul had assured Steve that once he had taken care of these fine fellows, the vital license permitting embarkation would be issued.

Mentally calculating the amounts of gold bullion we would have to extract from purchasers of each bit of our fern, we sent more money. Daily we waited to hear that our treasure was on its way on the high seas. Daily Albert sat staring at the phone. And after several weeks, a final letter from Steve arrived. Not having heard from Raoul since forwarding him the funds, Steve had journeyed to the port. There he found the Customs office closed, and was told that everybody was at the fiesta which had been going on for the past three weeks under the sponsorship of the Customs officers.

Our fern was piled on the dock. There, as far as we know, it is still piled.

But we mourned it not. After all, did we not have the satisfaction of knowing that we had raised the gross national product of our neighbor to the south at least several percentage points?

Trapping the Wild Orchid

Plant sales were the guts of the B&B business, and the more plants we sold, the more plants we needed. Patsy labored long to divide every plant as soon as it was dividable, and Albert presided at the conception and birth of innumerable new hybrids. But Birst & Borpling's reputation was built on species orchids, nature's originals which had evolved without artificial insemination and required no sword of Solomon to multiply.

When I mentioned our need for some new and exciting species, Albert pointed languidly to a drawer down at the bottom of his desk. I opened it with difficulty, for it was jammed with unopened letters. They were postmarked from places with unpronounceable names in South America, Central America, and the farthest reaches of Asia. Everyone of them contained lists of

Incomprehensible dialect

orchids, which the writer had collected from the jungle and was honored to offer to the esteemed purveyor of rarities in the land of the free and the home of the brave orchid grower. Here and there we found a note from an expatriate American, a hermit who we pictured as an ape-like creature swinging through the trees seeking orchids to go with his bananas.

We spent hours poring over the letters and consulting orchid books to verify the plant descriptions, which were usually more flowery than accurate. Albert helped by telling us that the dried-out plants shipped by the Koong Fooy Nursery in Zoomoo Province never survived the fumigation at the port of entry here, or that no plant shipped by Orinoco Oskar was ever correctly labeled.

He had high praise, however, for two or three collectors, so we sent orders to them. And after a few weeks, we were calling a trucking company to pick up batches of casket-like crates at the inspection station at the airport. Patsy pretended to be disgruntled by this influx of "junk," but we noticed that he carefully eyeballed each plant and tenderly tucked it into just the right pot.

One of our collectors, a former Maine lobsterman trans-planted to Nicaragua, proved to be a fascinating correspondent. Benny regaled us with tales of sending his crew of naked native boys swarming up into giant trees, gleefully swinging their machetes and sending great clumps of orchids hurtling to the ground.

A casual remark in one of Benny's letters mystified us. "I had a visit yesterday from two gals from Old Macdonald's Farm," he wrote. "I gave them the Albert treatment, and they went away happy."

Albert enlightened us. "Oh, that's just the EIEIO, the Energetic Individuals for Environmental Interests Organization. They go around making sure nobody is raping Mother Nature."

"And just what is the Albert treatment?," I asked.

"Well, you take the ladies on a special tour. Not too far, because you don't want them getting their Abercrombie and Fitch safari clothes dusty. You show them how you very gently pry only tiny pieces off the biggest clumps of plants. You have tears in your eyes, and you beg the plants' forgiveness for disturbing them.

"Works every time. But I can't take credit for this little stratagem. I learned it from an old collector who got religion and put away the elephant gun he used to use on unwanted visitors."

He smiled benignly on us, and said, "Let's tell Benny we can use another shipload of plants. I know he'll find them if there are any left."

Honeymooning With Orchids

Customers and friends who went abroad often gave Albert plants they brought home from their travels. One such gift he especially treasured, not because the plants were great but because their story was.

Sue and Lew Bennett had just been married. For their honeymoon, they chose an orchid tour in Guyana (then called Guiana). Not just an ordinary orchid hunting odyssey, but a grand tour led by the famous Jose Bragganzarosa. Senor Bragganzarosa knew where to find orchids in remote areas seldom visited by the most avid plant explorers.

Sue never spoke of the trip after the divorce, but Lew made it conversational fodder for a lifetime. One letter he wrote to Albert demonstrated his delight.

"Jose took us to the virtually unexplored Cockerboo country. It's just a blank on the map. We trekked through places with names that translated to 'District of Look Behind' and 'Me No See, You No Come.' It's very eerie; even the light seems different, and the natives speak an incomprehensible dialect while waving their poisoned spears at tourists. The orchids in the trees are gorgeous but unfortunately rather inaccessible since the region is strangely lacking in rescue squads to save those who slip from the branches and go over the cliffs."

The fauna, he reported, was as fascinating as the flora. Jose was adept at spotting the ubiquitous poisonous snake. When he encountered the occasional pfoof beetle – so called because "one bite and pfoof, no more you" – he dispatched it with an unerring stream of tobacco juice.

Jose also had minor fame as a medicine man. When Sue reached into a banyan tree to pluck a shy orchid, only to fall with an unseemly screech into a nettle vine, he was quick to apply a foul-smelling mud to ease the pain of the hundreds of tiny hypodermic needles piercing her posterior. Sue stopped moaning in only a few hours, and the happy trio was able to continue hacking their way through the lovely jungle.

Only a few minor disappointments marred their idyll. Some beautiful orchids inhabited thorny thickets, and the travelers regretted forgetting to bring their suits of armor. One exquisite orchid was discovered thriving on a gravelly hillside, but Jose reported that it did not like being disturbed, and survival of the plants was likely only if one carefully carted off most of the hillside.

Despite a few trivial mishaps – such as when Sue leaned over a waterfall and the bank crumbled beneath her (she was found two days later clinging to a rock that looked like a sleeping crocodile) – Lew's happiness never flagged. He only confessed a momentary puzzlement at Sue's refusal to speak to him from her stretcher on the plane coming home, when he announced that they would be taking an orchid tour on every anniversary, but to much more exciting places.

Beautiful orchids came from thorny thickets.

Chapter 7

Talking To Myself

"Oh joy! Oh ecstasy!" Betty cried as she slammed down the phone.

"The Ladybugs and Slugs Garden Club wants to learn about orchids. They are inviting us to lecture to them on Saturday. And not only do we get free eats, they have found seven dollars in their treasury to pay us."

"Oh joy, indeed," I growled. "Well, I'm not bringing any plants this time. Nobody buys any, and I end up lugging them all home again. I'll run off something on the mimeo, maybe just an invitation to visit the greenhouses and directions on how to get here. On second thought, maybe not – they might actually come."

This was only our third or fourth voyage on the lecture circuit, but already we were beginning to feel unappreciated.

As I may have mentioned, Albert loved to talk. The great tragedy of his life, at least to hear him tell it, was being unable to talk to everyone everywhere. His numerous ailments of feet, back, prostate and proboscis kept him from greatest love, lecturing (especially to garden clubs, which invariably consisted of ladies who listened raptly to his every charm-oozing word).

But now he had two personable and persuadable people to carry the torch.

"You'll meet some great people, and you'll sell lots of plants. And besides," he paused impressively, "you'll get to dine out. They serve really great meals after a lecture."

This decided us, we being gourmets frustrated because we had no time for gourmanding. We got out Albert's old projector and dived into the thousands of color slides he kept in shoe boxes. While Betty spouted the joys of growing orchids, I would operate the projector and throw in an enthusiastic comment now and then. We worked out a conversational style that could not fail to generate mass drooling for our wares.

Alas, out fervor began to waver after our very first lecture stint. We addressed a local men's garden club, a hale and hearty

The Outhouse Lecture

group of businessmen who left their business cares behind once a month to chat about growing green things other than currency. Their competitive spirit, however, was not left behind, since their conversation before the lecture revolved around whose roses were rosier or whose magnolia flowers were huger.

We did sell a couple of plants at that meeting, though not to the gentleman who said he had tried orchids in his greenhouse. All through our talk, he grunted and snorted whenever we showed a slide of an orchid that was notoriously easy to grow. Curious, we confronted this scoffer after the meeting.

This was our first encounter with a phytocidal maniac, a serial killer of plants. He was oblivious to the fact that plants had needs. He hung shade lovers to roast near the roof of his greenhouse, and those that required maximum sun went under the benches. His philosophy? "They grow in jungles, don't they? Nobody fusses over them there, do they?"

We did meet some charming people, but almost always found that their interest in plants was vicarious. They loved hearing about how others grew this and that, but confined their own efforts to the hollyhocks Grandmother grew or window boxes of those darling geraniums.

We lectured in private homes, parish houses, firehouses, and cocktail lounges where the clink of ice and glasses accompanied our shouted sentences. Once we imparted our wisdom in the yard of a farmhouse with a creaky pump and an outhouse making a bucolic background. Plumbing, by the way, could be a problem when lecturing in some homes. When one is rapturously extolling the beauty of an orchid, it is a little disconcerting to have one's words punctuated by repeated flushings of a toilet behind the nearest wall.

Partake At Your Peril

"Dining out" on the lecture trail was apt to be either glorious or gory. We were feted with borscht and blintzes, with delectable fare from Casa Cloudyskies (Mandarin/Mesopotamian cuisine), with Seven-Up and Cheese Doodles, and on one great occasion, with giant pastrami-on-ryes with really good beer.

Then there was the endless parade of potluck suppers where everyone brought a favorite dish, the only criterion for which was total unrecognizability of ingredients. We had many a merry game on the way home guessing, "What the hell were we eating?"

The gods of the kitchen, Indie and Gestion, ruled supreme in suburbia. After several uncomfortable intestinal incidents, we learned to plead various ailments and allergies that prevented us from partaking of any dish we could not identify. Albert, of course, was always sympathetic. "Well, if you must make pigs of yourselves…"

One church supper was particularly memorable. After our lecture, we were approaching the festive board, when the group's president sidled up to us. In a whisper, she confided, "We're all hoping you'll be sure to compliment Eulalia on the food, because it's the first time we have let her cook for us since the INCIDENT" (she barely breathed the word).

Our cranial computers digested this enigmatic statement, but they took a few minutes to spit out the answer. Once again we saw the headlines of several years ago: "Church Supper Fells 58"…"Casserole Catastrophe." "Tri-County Disaster Plan Put To Test." We recalled the mobilization of dozens of rescue squads, the first mass evacuation by helicopter of the afflicted to distant hospitals, and one of the most exhaustive investigations ever conducted by the Centers of Disease Control. Eulalia's cooking had brought her fame never dreamed of by Lucrezia Borgia's press agent.

I seemed to recall that all had survived New England's most famous case of mass food poisoning. Nevertheless, a glacier took up residence in my stomach. I looked at Betty.

"Number Four?" she whispered. "Oh, yes, yes, yes," I quavered back. It was time for Contingency Plan Number Four. We sauntered over to the table and helped ourselves to paper plates. Suddenly, I dropped my plate and struck my head a mighty blow. I screamed, "My God, I forgot to activate the fertigator on the vuyletekearas!"

Giving me her best "How could you, you fiend" look, Betty whirled and shrieked to the assemblage, "Gotta go, gotta go terrible emergency at the greenhouses – thank you, thank, you, thank you!"

We exited like does pursued by Sasquatch, and never looked back. A few miles down the road, Betty said, "Geez, I was hungry, but now the bubble gum and hominy grits in our fridge look really good."

Lecher Self Go

There was one church social we really enjoyed, though not its aftermath. The church – more like a cathedral – was in the most upper upper class community in the state, and our old station wagon seemed to shrink in shame when wedged in among the magnificent conveyances that thronged the parking lot.

The catered fete that preceded our lecture was sumptuous but fortunately calorie-light, so it did not induce the soporific state which all too often assailed speaker and audience alike when lecture followed food. Indeed, the congregation actually appeared to be listening to our talk, and even asked an intelligent question or two at its conclusion.

When we stepped down from the podium, a congratulatory crowd surged around us. But almost immediately, the sea parted to allow the passage of two giants. Deacon Fuller Filbert and his wife Felicia were obviously pillars of the church, in form as well as function. They towered over everybody else, and everybody else glowed like stars in the reflected radiance of these glorious suns.

Felicia enfolded Betty in a smothering hug, and Fuller pumped my hand and boomed, "Superb! Most inspiring!" He clapped his arm around my shoulder. "In fact, my dear fellow, I'm so inspired that I am going to be so bold as to ask a very small favor of you."

He lowered his voice to impart a confidence. "Felicia and I have a small greenhouse and a few orchids. We would be deeply in your debt if you would visit and advise us on expanding our collection.

"Patting my arm, he administered the coup de grace. "Over cocktails and dinner, of course. And we have just installed a modest but delightful swimming pool, so by all means bring your bathing suits."

On the appointed day, we snaked our way up the Filberts' endless driveway. I parked behind a fire-engine-red roadster, which I recognized as one of those little European jobs with thunderbolts under the hood.

The Deacon had obviously done well for himself on Wall
Street. The Filbert domicile was the usual massive turreted
Tudor mandated by the town's zoning laws. It failed, however, to
dwarf the "small greenhouse", a towering structure of gleaming
glass and impressive circumference. And the new swimming
pool made us envy the pool cleaners who couldn't help but get
rich keeping its sea and shores sparkling.

Fuller and Felicity greeted us with casual waves, and soon
we were ensconced on chaise lounges around the pool. Drinks
and canapés were served by the Filberts' sole domestic staff.
Fuller divulged that "our man Ramon," who he had discovered
working as a bouncer in a gay bar in the Bronx, was a Paris-
trained chef who had also been the toast of Muscle Beach.
Ramon sported bulging biceps from his cheeks down to his

ankles. Attired in shining purple shorts and a bile-green beret, he never smiled, but his piercing eyes were ever alert to our every libational and gustatory need.

A pleasant hour passed chatting about orchids. Then Felicity suggested that we all retire to the pool house to don our bathing suits. When we emerged, everyone jumped into the pool.

Almost immediately, the Filberts began exhibiting hidden talents for uninhibited playfulness. This was not a place for swimming, but for ducking, tossing and tumbling guests of the opposite sex. Felicity would dive down and pull me under, then rescue me in a tight embrace of arms, legs and toes. Betty, too, was introduced to underwater contact sports. When she found Fuller's hands going where none but her husband's had gone before, she headed for the ladder to exit the pool.

Fuller and Felicity followed us onto the deck. Neither of them seemed to notice that we shied away from them as if they had chainsaws for hands.

"Oh, what fun," Felicity cried. "And wouldn't it be even more fun if we got rid of these horrid suits?"

Fuller chimed in, "What a great idea! So unnecessary, things like clothes, don't you agree? And after all, we won't want to be burdened with any when we play games among the orchids after dinner.

"It finally dawned on us. The Deacon and his consort were swingers. They swung and swapped as gleefully as children throwing candy at each other at a party.

We had no contingency plan for this one. Betty improvised with an attack of acute orchidomania. "Orchids? You want to grow orchids? You're crazy, just like all the rest of them," she shrieked, rolling her eyes in her head.

I backed up this brilliant performance by moaning, "My God, it's happening again. We're not safe when she's like this."

I heaved her up onto my shoulder, and staggered to the pool house for our clothes, then to the car, wishing I had left the motor running. We left Fuller and Felicity staring after us, still wearing their suits if not their haloes. We had not seen, much less sold, an orchid, but we could always say that we had experienced life in the fastest lane.

Shut Up and Sit Down

I know you will be surprised to hear that right after the Filbert fracas, we put out feet and rumps down and told Albert, "No more!" We decreed that hereafter we would lecture only to orchid societies, and maybe once in a while to one of the big horticultural societies who just might have a member or two who was interested in plants. Poison, peril and pestilence lurked on the lecture trail. Yes, we had learned our lesson.

Or rather, several lessons. One was taught to us by a wise old nurseryman. "For forty years," he said, "I wrote and wrote, and talked, talked and talked about plants. I finally got it into my head that people preferred to be told face-to-face than on paper, because it is easier to forget something they hear than something they read." Which we took to mean that the pen is mightier than the voice, and writer's cramp puts more in the bank than aching vocal cords.

However, if you should happen to aspire to mouth your way to fame and fortune, you might want to chew on this advice which Betty wrote to a friend who was terrified by the thought of mounting a lecture platform.

"Anyone can be a great lecturer," she wrote. "All it takes is to remember you're there to ENTERTAIN.

"You are not educating, preaching, or proselytizing. You are giving a performance, and you had damn well better make it worthy of a Broadway stage even if you're standing next to an outhouse.

"So speak up, put drama in your gestures, and make the uninteresting sound like the pronouncements of a prophet on a mountain top. And never never stop for a second to think how you are doing. Be unflappable, and the audience will see you as an AUTHORITY. They'll never know you are quaking with butterflies in the gut and claustrophobia of the throat."

I agreed with this, but it seemed to me that she had left out the greatest secret of the successful lecturer.

Actually, it's an old adage, we learned from Albert, though only by example. He never articulated it, but he practiced it to perfection. "If you can't dazzle them with brilliance, baffle them with bullshit."

Chapter 8

The Merry Men and Winsome Women of MNTOS

Albert pestered us to join the big regional orchid society, where, he said, everything was happening. Everybody who was anybody in the orchid world belonged to the Metropolitan Northern Tier Orchid Society, popularly known as MNTOS (min-toss).

MNTOS was the usual mix of democracy, aristocracy, and guerilla warfare one finds in any not-for-profit organization. Commoners who grew orchids on windowsills mingled with landed gentry with gargantuan greenhouses. The twain met, and the cauldron bubbled, with liberal stirrings by many who put on airs even though they could not afford them.

The Society's Secretary.

MNTOS' great leader was a gentleman named Valentino Porsche. President P, as he liked to be called, collected presidencies. He had attained the highest office in a score of horticultural organizations. A retired advertising mogul who had achieved crown-and-scepter status in his profession, President P ruled MNTOS with a blend of teddy bear charm and gangster force.

President P displayed his split personality in lightning flashes. One moment he would be bestowing lavish praise on one of his subjects, in the next he was snarling to another, "How did you ever manage to come up with such a half-baked crazy idea?" These chameleon changes never failed to entrance us, for President P was completely "average" in appearance, his only distinguishing characteristics being a huge head with a very small nose and very big eyes.

President P and Vice President Chauncey Dickerson Smythe (who had been Charlie Smith before he became the first wizard of telemarketing) were master politicians who effortlessly inveigled everyone to their way of thinking at MNTOS Board of Directors meetings. President P would run an idea up the flagpole thusly: "My extensive and intensive in-depth research indicates that we can escalate the Society prestige-wise by infiltrating the non-orchid-oriented public to activate its latent status desire impulse."

V.P. Smythe would reply, "Sir, your concept shapes up methodologically, but I would suggest that we maximize the deployment of achievers in our group who have attained the ultimate in cultural superiority so as to efficaciously expedite our goal attainment."

Since no one knew what they were talking about, the motion passed unanimously. A board member was once heard to remark, "Give us a few more like those two, and we can destroy civilization." The Society's Secretary, a mouse with mammoth shorthand skills, dipped frequently into the cooking sherry while trying to decipher her notes on the pontifications of these potentates. And the Treasurer, an octogenarian who roused from stupor only when the word "money" was spoken, reserved his most heartfelt snore for their orations.

Brotherhood of the Pseudobulb

Any other conglomeration of joiners, MNTOS was constantly seething with intrigue. President P and Vice President Smythe outdid the CIA in covert operations aimed at making MNTOS an exclusive entity open only to the most accomplished (meaning monied) orchidists. An opposing faction took the Haight-Ashbury approach and sought to make MNTOS an open society of free thinkers and free lovers (horticulturally speaking, of course). Still another group thought the refreshments were the main purpose of meetings, and always brought gleaming silver flasks to enhance their coffee and donuts.

Most of the time, Betty and I managed to remain neutral in these machinations. We became observers, adroitly avoiding the controversial while marveling at the fascinating facets of human nature.

We got to know the amateur hybridizer who named his creations for many of his friends, but never one after his wife because if it turned out to be a dog his life wouldn't be worth living. We delighted in watching the little leprechaun who oversaw acres of greenhouses on the estate of a financier. He was always accompanied by his greenhouse crew, a bevy of long-legged and impressively endowed beauties, and he was devastated when they all disappeared after a plague of giant cockroaches invaded the greenhouses.

We avoided the couple who had been spitting acid at each other for at least forty of their thirty years of marriage. Both were gifted with tongues that could take the paint off a barn at fifty paces. But they saw themselves as the happiest of couples, and unleashed fusillades of vitriol on the hapless soul who sought to smooth things over.

A couple everyone wanted but never got to know were Jack and Elvira Trembly. Founders of MNTOS and other local orchid societies in states from Minnesota to Arizona where they had homes, the Tremblys were the bluest of bluebloods. They were both in their nineties, and notable for their total lack of both smiles and loquaciousness, probably because their faces were so wrinkled such acts would have made them crumble.

Everyone wanted to meet the Founders.

Tall and gaunt, they resembled praying mantises. Jack tended to mumble, but in a deep and rasping voice like a displeased lion. Elvira would peer at everything through her lorgnette, with all the horror of a New York City water inspector finding typhoid in his microscope.

The Tremblys were the stuff of legend, and although one Mntosian was heard to say that they had all the charm of starving piggies, when they entered the meeting hall we seemed to hear the braying of trumpets and had to resist an urge to prostrate ourselves in obeisance. Little was known of Elvira, except that her vast wealth was said to have been derived from an ancestor who had invented the condom. At 95, Jack's eyes still lit up at the sight of a pretty girl, and it was rumored that he had had a harem when eight years old. When not appraising the female scenery, his eyes almost disappeared into his head, giving him such a pained look that president P said that poor old Jack must be suffering from croissant withdrawal.

MNTOS also had several unofficial officers. Robby Jones was the self-appointed MNTOS photographer. He took slides of everyone and everything at meetings, and lived well on the proceeds of their sale. Tall and thin as a flower stem, Robby had shrubs for eyebrows and a mustache as wide as his shoulders. Betty called him The Wraith, but he was more popularly known as The S. O. B. because of his habit of sidling up behind a show table exhibitor and murmuring, "Slide, old boy?"

Robby was the meekest of men. Only once did he clash with anyone. Doc Billie Corcoran brought more plants to the monthly show table than anyone else, and he was wont to see symptoms of dread diseases in any plant which won a higher award than his own and demand its immediate destruction.

Doc Billie took his own pictures, and he often pushed Robby aside when they were clicking shutters near each other. One day Robby stood it no longer. His handlebar mustache quivering, he drew himself up to his full seven feet and squeaked, "Sir, I am not a fly to be brushed away by the tail on a horse's ass."

Doc Billie was astounded. After all, wasn't he not only the perfect gentleman, but also a benefactor of the orchid world who shared his vastly superior plants by selling tiny divisions which needed triage treatment to survive, for only ten times what they were worth?

Such disputes were usually mediated by the society's self-appointed hostess. Lucinda Gulppe was what we call a revolving door orchidist – she bought only plants which were about to bloom, and when the flowers wilted she sent them out the door of her Greenwich Village apartment while new ones with bursting buds came in the same door. She dressed beautifully, in flowered off-the-shoulder outfits and shiny gold boots, and her pure-platinum hair was coiffed in authentic Swahili headdress fashion.

Lucinda was a greeter extraordinaire. Every new member or guest at a meeting became a dignitary deserving the red carpet of her lilting voice. It would rise above the tumult, "Oh, my dear, how wonderful of you to come. Let me introduce you to everyone. And do have some of my goodies" (she was renowned for her little rock cakes made with real rocks and coffee which compared favorably with oozings from a primeval swamp.

Lucinda was everywhere, providing tissues for the sinus-impaired and cushions for tender tushies. She also volunteered, gaily taking on tasks for absent or incapacitated menials. Once, just once, when we were unable to attend a meeting, we asked Lucinda to record the show table awards so we could report them in the society's newsletter. We received six pages of hieroglyphs inscribed on ledger sheets which apparently had been put through a blender. Betty threw up (her hands), and snarled, "What does she think we're running – a Dead Sea Scrolls operation?" I could only suggest meekly that we should never again miss a meeting even if we had to crawl down the turnpike and ford the river clinging to straws of osmunda fiber.

Publish and Perish

Lucinda had only one rival for the adulation of the MNTOS masses. Delilah Corpus was a widow whose husband Hubert had left her with only a few reams of IBM stock certificates, a 39-room cottage, and a block-long greenhouse of orchids.

Everyone had to – and I mean had to – admire Delilah. Though she exuded it from every pore, she never said, "Poor little me." Only rarely – never more than five or six times an hour – did she bemoan her awful problems keeping domestic help, especially nannies for her three children, all of whom apparently aspired to the best education reform schools had to offer. Her only comfort was her orchids, or more correctly, her orchid grower, one Archie McGrabbitt, a man of many green thumbs and an unquenchable thirst for fine Scotch and beautiful women who paid large salaries for playing with orchids.

Delilah had one great talent. She was an organizer. From the moment she joined MNTOS, she saw how desperately we needed to "cozy up" the seating arrangements at our meetings, how vital it was to have a make-up artist to embellish our speakers' visages, and how our show table required designing with the artistry of an exhibition being staged at the White House. Her frequent, "Don't you think we should..." inspired lemming-like urges to hurl oneself over a cliff.

After their first meeting, in which each strove to out-coo the other, Lucinda and Delilah worked tirelessly to avoid being at the same end of the room at the same time. Between them milled a horde of members performing intricate dances to keep themselves as far as possible from the contenders. Occasionally a member would reel when grazed by one of the darts of molten hatred flying across the room. Being an accomplished arbitrator, President P devised a solution that brought about a cease fire. He suggested that the ladies "co-guest edit" an issue of the society's monthly newsletter.

Orchid Bits (the word bytes had not been invented yet) had been Betty's baby for several years. She kept it simple, usually just eight pages long, a chatty mix of society news and short articles on orchid plants and people. Nothing hard about it, and President P was right. The girls loved the idea, and the dove of peace descended.

The great guest issue, however, was a little slow to appear. Five months later, each member received a parcel delivered by a panting postman. Bound in imitation Moroccan leather, it was a

167-page tome with its cover emblazoned with the names of its editors several times the size of its title.

It contained lots of society news, such as what was served when the so-and-sos visited the whosises, and whose butler had been seen sneaking into his mistress' bedchamber in the wee hours. Recipes with two-page lists of ingredients were featured along with detailed instructions for making flower arrangements with orchids nobody had ever heard of. Equally fascinating were articles such as the 17-page dissertation by the Lithuanian biologist who had discovered fossils of a giant prehistoric moth which pollinated a long-extinct miniature orchid in Sierra Leone.

President P called an emergency meeting of the board of directors to deal with the mass resignations, libel suits, and bankruptcy proceedings necessitated by the printer's bill. Though gallows and drawing-and-quartering were mentioned frequently, the board settled on a letter of congratulations to be sent to the editors, stressing that never again would the society trouble them to undertake such a masterwork. They had achieved the impossible, and we hoped that they would share their superb gifts with many other organizations in dire need of their incomparable talents (the phrase, "preferably in Outer Mongolia", was deleted from the final draft).

The Speaker Spouts

Lest you suspect that MNTOS meetings were devoted only to posturing and pillaging, let me assure you that the speakers each months were always interesting and sometimes unforgettable.

This was due to our Program Chairwoman. Cissy Bodenblitxer was so successful in digging up (sometimes almost literally) exciting speakers that it was inevitable that she would hold the office of P. C. as long as she wanted it. A mini-mouse of the horn-rim-spectacles and hair-in-a-bun type, Cissy was super-efficient, handling with aplomb every detail from making hotel reservations for visiting lecturers to seeing that they arrived at the meeting place well fed and on time. She accomplished all

this while working as a systematic botanist at a botanical garden
and writing an 800-page monograph on an extremely rare orchid.

An admirable person, indeed. But suddenly, Cissy
transformed. Upon reaching a certain almost-middle age, she
"bloomed." Gone were the tailored suits and sturdy shoes. The
new Cissy appeared in Indian saris or Guatemalan peasant
dresses adorned with tons of jangling jewelry. She forsook any
hint of make-up, and her rather large feet were sheathed in
sandals even in January.

Cissy became a magnet for every bachelor and widower in the Society, and we could hear her constant cries of delight, which Betty said sounded like the shrieks of a parrot having its tail feathers pulled out. Once we overheard her telling a rapt audience how she had thrown out most of the orchids in her greenhouse and replaced them with frogs. Her favorites were the green tree frogs known as axolotis, which she named for all her relatives, and she bemoaned her problem of getting enough maggots to feed them. I couldn't help wishing that she would kiss one of them so he would turn into a prince and carry her off to his castle.

On the night of the great blackout of 1965, Cissy, President P and V. P. Smythe had shown up early to get ready for the meeting in the banquet hall where MNTOS congregated. When the lights went out, they decided not to join the throngs marching up the avenues chanting, "We'll make the Bronx tonight!" They stayed in the hall all night, and kept room service hopping to supply them with liquid fortitude. When the hotel security officer checked the hail at 2 a. m., he found the trio singing, "Throw out the Lifeline" as their last candle sputtered out. The next morning, all three agreed that it was the best meeting MNTOS had ever had.

Seekers of the Wild Orchid

Among Cissy's most popular programs were the tales told by members about their adventures in search of orchids in their natural habitats. No continent had been neglected by intrepid Mntosians as they scoured the world in search of the elusive masdevallia and odontioda.

The Simptons always drew a huge crowd. They were truly the giants of orchid hunters. This is a literal description. At meetings, Will and Hortensia each occupied two chairs, and airlines the world over were known to demand they pay for two or even three seats apiece. Nevertheless, they had great stamina, and with the aid of sturdy burros, camels and litter bearers they traversed the wilds of far lands with great gusto and unbounded joy.

Since Will was unable to speak for long without wheezing, it was Hortensia who told our assemblage the stories of their travels. Neither lacked for courage. When Hortensia fell into a deep and fast-moving stream in an Australian gorge, Will promptly jumped in and acted as a dam to divert the current until she could be roped and hauled out.

In Africa, Hortensia was almost pulped by a charging bull elephant. She didn't get out of the way until the last second because she thought it was Will coming through the brush.

One of Will's most horrendous perils occurred when the happy couple was being driven in an ancient Hispano-Suiza taxi in Indonesia. Will had the misfortune to remark to the driver, a French expatriate named Bonaparte Leboubier, that he thought De Gaulle was doing a remarkable job of restoring France to its former glory.

Bonaparte, however, considered De Gaulle to be a monster who was destroying his homeland. He accelerated, weaving wildly through dense traffic with rarely a hand on the wheel. When the Hispano-Suiza finally expired in a cloud of smoke and steam, Will and Hortensia clambered out and, probably for the only time in their lives, ran, cheered on by hordes who were delighted by the Gallic madman and his elephantine fares.

Nothing ever really fazed the Simptons. On a trip to Guatemala, they were ferried into the interior by Over the Jordan Airlines, which consisted of one single-engine airplane of early World War II vintage. The pilot confided that he occasionally made unscheduled flights to see his friend Fidel in Cuba. His wife served as stewardess whenever he carried important passengers like the Simptons. The only others on board were three Latin lover types who never spoke during the flight. They spent the time casting longing looks at the pilot's wife, but were seemingly deterred from pursuing her acquaintance by the huge single-action Colt the pilot wore in a shoulder holster.

Will and Hortensia enjoyed the ride immensely, even joining the pilot in resounding cries of "Yippie!" whenever the plane dived precipitously into a valley after scraping a mountain top.

The high point of the trip was when the plane's door suddenly flew open. The pilot nonchalantly banked steeply to the other side so that the door slammed shut, but not before a nearly full case of tequila went hurtling out into the beyond. Not a single "Yippie!" was heard for the rest of the flight.

The Great White Orchid Hunter

If you could afford it, you took the Cadillac of orchid tours. You hired yourself off to Brazil, to be escorted by the one-and-only Bub Belcher. Only a privileged few Mntosians had ever done this, and their recountings of "doing it with Bub" always made one of Cissy's truly great meeting programs.

This denizen of the Amazonian jungles was said to know every inch of the terrain for hundreds of miles in every direction from his abode high in a baobab tree. With his Charlton Heston countenance, enormous crown of salt-and pepper hair and down-to-his-waist beard, he could have passed for any of the Biblical prophets, except that instead of flowing robes, he was invariably attired in the very latest a-hunting-we-will-go outfit decreed by the best men's fashion magazines.

Bub had two kinds of tours. If he liked you – which meant (a) you were as comely as he was, and (b) you understood or at least pretended to understand his mix of Oxford English and native dialects – you got to see the finest scenery and the best orchids. If he didn't care for you, you trekked twice as far and saw half as much.

One reason Bub's tours were fabulously expensive was his insistence that the tourist purchase from him certain items which were absolutely vital to success and survival. He had curved daggers with jeweled handles which he said were far superior to any knife for cutting orchid plants out of trees. Every tourist also had to have a large bag, of the finest leather, with straps for carrying over the shoulder and velvet-lined compartments for transporting the day's catch of orchids in comfort (he didn't say whether he meant the comfort of the plants or of the carrier).

One essential piece of equipment was a state-of-the-art hearing aid. His clients thought this was necessary to enhance their enjoyment of the jungle's bird and animal sounds, but he dissuaded them of this notion. "You keep this turned up about halfway, and you'll hear any crocodiles creeping up behind you. And when we go through certain places, you'll want it at full power so you can hear the big snakes slithering along the branches over your head before they latch on to you."

No crocs or boa constrictors were sighted at close range on Bub's tours, and those that he spotted in the distance apparently, had such marvelous camouflage abilities that they disappeared before binoculars could be focused on them. Nevertheless, everyone lucky enough to be guided by Bub Belcher always came home with great tales of near encounters with monstrous though unseen jungle creepers and crawlers.

Binoculars were permitted, but no one but Bub was allowed to carry a camera. "Too many get damaged when you have to dive for cover from a charging boar," he explained. When you wanted a picture, you'd tell Bub and he obliged. Admittedly, he was a fine photographer, and several weeks later you received a parcel of magnificent prints from his nephew, an air-brush expert for *Playboy Magazine*, and no one could be so brash as to complain about their astronomical cost.

Wild boar alert!

"Win, you bastard, win!"

Chapter 9

Crazed Chlorophyll

Many a wise man has never been able to explain the fascination orchids hold for the human animal, but let me try.

You might say that the beauty of their flowers is reason enough for growing them, and we won't argue that the thrill of blooming even an "ordinary" orchid brings a pounding of the heart and a swelling of the bosom. But to the true orchidist, this nothing, nothing, a negligible and totally irrelevant rationalization for a passion that goes far deeper.

The cultivation of orchids is the supreme ego trip. Even a minor success confers a high that elevates one above his fellows to become a god in the heavens. The key phrase is "above his fellows," for the dedicated orchidist is seeking (though he would never admit it) POWER. He wants to be able to say, "So he won a Nobel Prize. I bloomed a *Phragmipedium exstaminidium*."

Not even the amassing of great wealth matches this glow. And such ecstasy can be yours in many ways. Imagine the awe of the uninitiated when they hear you carrying on an entire conversation in botanical Latin, interspersed with an occasional explosive "Superb!" or slightly more muted "How awful!" You are admired for your precise descriptions of flowers: a flower is never red, it is fuchsia, cerise, blood, mauve, maroon or Mandarin, and a yellow bloom must be bullion gold or suffused with autumn sunlight or subtle hints of peachy-peach.

The urge to undo all others is unleashed in those normally the most modest of persons. Every meeting of two or more orchid growers is an arena of gladiators out for blood. The windowsill grower who exhibits a plant with more flowers than a plant of the same species shown by a greenhouse grower feels deserving of a ticker tape parade up Broadway. Behind every real orchidist we have ever known stands an invisible coach screaming, "Win, you bastard, win!"

Should your spouse take off with a new love, your orchid genes will rise and enable you to reaffirm your worth through your vastly superior appreciation of a much higher form of life. Don't we all realize that orchids are the most highly evolved of all plants, and does not one who knows and grows them soar, despite all the tribulations life has thrown at him, to heights far above all others in the human firmament?

What's In A Name?

... Power, passion, fame, fortune, and probably much more. To have a new species or hybrid named for one, of course, ensures a place in posterity, even though future owners of the plant will likely have no idea who you were. But for more permanent ego boosting, nothing beats a knowledge of orchid nomenclature. The specialist in this is known as a taxonomist, and he or she inhabits the loftiest peaks of orchidom.

If you are conversant with a few hundred of the more than 25,000 species of orchids, you are an AUTHORITY. This is a title that must be jealously guarded and defended with rapier and catapult against those who would be considered a higher, i.e., more authoritative, authority than you. Maintaining your eminence requires copious scrupulous research and frequent publication of unintelligible monographs read only by other taxonomists.

In 1957, an international committee consisting of several dozen experts was established to formulate rules for naming and registering orchids. This monumental task was meant to ensure correct identification of all the orchids in existence, and it was hailed as a great aid to everyone growing, showing or dealing in orchids. Some said it would even save lives, for nothing is more likely to cause suicidal shame than having an incorrectly labeled plant.

Unfortunately, the great work did nothing to end the Hundred Years War of the Taxonomists. Become an expert on Oncidium, Epidendrum or Maxillaria, and you face the ire and arrows of outraged competitors who see themselves as the only true authority on the orchids in question. Many a shot fired in this war was heard round the world, and sometimes not just in

Some said that orchid naming rules would save lives.

the rarified air of the technical journal. A program chairman in one orchid society was fired when he invited two taxonomists who happened to be in town at the same time to discuss their work in a joint program. This turned from a debate into a shouting match into a brawl worthy of a saloon in the Old West.

Shared goals and camaraderie, you may have gathered, were unknown in this world. A hated B, B despised C, and D thought all three merited slow death by suffocation under masses of misnamed orchids. Retracting a misstatement was unthinkable, and the most humble request to do so deserved, if you were lucky, a wall of silence, and if you were unlucky, a firestorm of invective that questioned your ancestry as well as your intelligence.

Anyone caught in the middle of one of these battles was likely to be scarred for life. We became involved in one such clash of the Titans through our friendship-by-mail with a reclusive but effusive chef-turned-taxonomist who lived in a California town we were never able to find on a map.

Carter Criswell had been a prodigy in the culinary arts since he was old enough to boil water. "Carty" became known as a master chef throughout the West before he was twenty, but his career in cuisine came to an abrupt end as a result of a kitchen experiment with an extremely poisonous plant he had picked in his backyard. Stunned that a little green weed could cause the near-demise of such an exalted personage as himself, Carty turned to botany with the same zeal he had applied to concocting his designer dishes. And naturally, his desire to work with only the best led him to orchids.

Carty's Comeuppance

We first "met" Carty Criswell when he wrote to thank us for a complimentary review we had written on one of his books. He sent us a stack of articles for the MNTOS newsletter, all satisfyingly accurate and well written. Though he mentioned that he suffered from numerous allergies and was plagued with bouts of gout, Carty's output was prodigious. In addition to writing scores of articles on orchids each year, he published several newsletters with intriguing titles such as "The Rhynocostylis Review" and "Vonderul Vandas." And while he had a reputation for being a nitpicker and a hurler of verbal thunderbolts, he rarely objected to our editing of his articles, and his chiding when we misspelled an orchid name was gentle compared to the barbs he directed toward other evil-doers.

Our correspondence with Carty over several years filled a couple of file drawers. Betty found his sense of humor equal to her own. To Carty, the name given to a new species, *Scopologena verruculata*, "sounds like something that is afflicting my neighbor." A botanist known for never having to pay a hotel or restaurant bill on his travels was "the mooching schnook", and the editor who cloaked his massive ignorance of plants with reams of self-righteous ranting was referred to as "that saintly ass."

Betty suggested that, since she and Carty had such impressive talents for castrating the fatuous and phony, they should start a company called "Narsty Letters, Inc." Its letterhead would proclaim, "A snarl in every sentence, a sneer in every syllable." The idea fell through when they could not decide whether to charge by the number of pages or the amount of vituperation on each page.

Well, finally Carty wrote THE BOOK. In just over 1,000 pages, he described and dissected every orchid known and grown anywhere in the world; from the commonest cattleya to the species with aphrodisiacal qualities that certain New Guinea tribes used in their coming-of-age rituals. It was a masterwork, and we and many others thought it the most interesting yet practical reference any orchidist could own. We said so in the MNTOS newsletter, and reviewers all over the world were equally laudatory.

All but one. The editor of the most prestigious international orchid journal felt compelled, for reasons hidden in the swamp of orchid politics, to assign Carty's worst enemy to review the opus. A world-renowned (in his own estimation) taxonomist, Antonin Yukofsky was not a man to let such an opportunity to disembowel a competitor pass him by. He eviscerated the book as "a pretentious compilation of misinformation, full of nomenclatural indiscretions that defy comprehension, let alone elucidating a complex subject the author should know enough to leave to people who know something about it."

Battle was joined, and Carty found he had more friends than he knew. The offending editor received scores of letters asking how he could publish such a hatchet job, so shrill and sour that anyone could see it was born of pure spite. Yukofsky was called "the noodnik of nomenclature" and "the sniveling goulash", and several less complimentary names. At one time it was rumored that hordes bearing torches and pitchforks were besieging the Yusofsky citadel on the outskirts of Stupengrad. The rebuke we enjoyed most came from a famous author who grew a few orchids. He said simply, "Tut, tut, Mr. Yukofsky."

Through all this, Carty was strangely subdued. In his last letter to us, he confided, "You know, I think my subconscious wanted me to write the damn book just to get a rise out of old Yukofsky. Maybe it's my mission in life to bring out the stinker in people. And I have to admit that Yus is a pretty good taxonomist, as far as taxonomists go."

Sex Rears Its Gorgeous Head

The members of MNTOS still talk about – or refuse to talk about – a lecture given by an orchidist from England. Algernon "Algie" McWhiney was undistinguished, completely average in appearance. But when he began to speak, his voice boomed like the carillons of Big Ben, and his eyes flashed and leaped about like the flickering lightning that portends a fierce storm.

Algie's lecture was entitled, "Pollination Mechanisms in the Orchidaceae." An innocuous, sure-to-be-dull subject, but we all hoped this modest and gentle preacher type would breathe some life into it. Algie opened by showing slides of the many insects that pollinate orchids. Our eyes glazed at an endless parade bees, wasps, flies, butterflies and hummingbirds. Many of these, Algie told us, were truly democratic, performing their duties on a wide variety of orchids, but others restricted their operations to a single, apparently super-seductive, species. Algie also confided that a few flowers – a very few, he sneered – were "facultatively autogamous;" these despicable blooms were able to pollinate themselves and so they spurned the advances of winged suitors.

Then Algie warmed to his subject. He and the atmosphere became noticeably warmer as he showed slides of the pollinators at work. His voice rose as he commented on each slide. "Go, baby, go!" resounded through the hall. At the sight of a bee belaboring an unattractive flower, he bellowed, "Idiot! There are better fish in the sea!" Two moths contending for the favors of one flower were exhorted, "Make love, not war, you asses!"

The Program Chairwoman appeared to have stopped breathing. Several (though not many) of the ladies were attempting to cover their eyes and ears simultaneously, and one gal was assuaging her hyperventilation with great nasal draughts of hot pepper sauce.

We expected dead silence at the end of the lecture, but Algie was feted with an ovation such as never before had been accorded a speaker at MNTOS. Members who belonged to other orchid societies mobbed Algie to persuade him to impart his wisdom to their groups. Cissy was resuscitated and congratulated for her genius in securing such an educational speaker.

And President P, who usually shook hands perfunctorily with speakers after their lectures, was seen grasping both of Algie's hands, pumping them vigorously and crying, "Right on, old boy! Right on!"

This was not MNTOS' only foray into the deeper passions of orchid growing. So successful was the "Pollination" lecture that a few months later our heroic Program Chairwoman booked a French lady, Mme. Monique de la Brie. She was, Cissy announced (with the tiniest hint of a smirk), the fastest-rising botanist/biologist/taxonomist in Europe, and she knew we would agree (again that teensy smirk) that Mme. Monique deserved equal adulation here. Her topic was "Intergeneric Hybridizing: Why Do We Do It?"

We of sat back, preparing to pinch ourselves painfully should yawn or snore impend. Neither Monique's subject nor her appearance was promising. Betty, who was already mentally

Madame Monique

composing the program report for the MNTOS newsletter, said the only word she could think of to describe Mme. de la Brie was "prissy."

Monique began with an enraptured dissertation on the Latin names being given newly discovered species of orchids. She revealed shyly that she herself had discovered several new species while on a perilous, poorly financed and horribly cuisined expedition in Sumatra. She showed slides, obviously taken with a circa 1850 pinhole camera, of her *Stenchorhizus richelieuius*, *Putridia maupassantae* and *Smellotius de Gaullius*.

She was also fascinated by the marvelously evocative names being given to new orchid hybrids. Didn't we think 'Ham and Swiss' was the perfect name for a brassolaelio cattleya with purplish-pink and sickly-cream flowers? She lauded a breeder, one Gus Bustello, who gave his creations lovely names such as 'Bustamelon', 'Bustiferous' and 'Superbustagut', the last being a lady's-slipper orchid whose huge toad-like flowers seemed about to explode.

This was mildly interesting, and only a few complexions were turning red with efforts to stifle yawns. But then something changed. Monique's silken tone took on a steely temper. "However, ve must all be avare," she varned, "that we are promoting INCEST in our orchids."

She backed up this heinous charge with an indictment of current trends in orchid breeding. The modern hybridizer was going too far. He was conjoining brothers, sisters, aunts, uncles and the most distant cousins in a veritable orgy of miscegenation.

Overheated with indignation, Monique tore off her glasses and unpinned her hair. The jacket of her suit came next, to reveal a poured-on sleeveless sweater. Her slim skirt, which had a zipper that zipped from the bottom, was unzipped to startling heights.

She picked up a pointer and stabbed viciously at a series of slides flashing across the screen. This (Brassavola) plus this (Epidendrum) plus this (Sophronitis) plus this (Laelia) plus this (Cattleya) equals this (Rothara)." Her voice dropped to a venomous whisper as she leveled the pointer at the audience. "Mr. Roth, whoever he is, should be ashamed to have such a MONGREL named after him."

We all shrank back, aghast at the realization that by creating such beauties as the Rothara 'Meteor Showers' shown on the screen, we were contributing to the bastardization of our cherished orchids (still, the idea of all those dogs sporting merrily with each other was a little exciting).

Monique strode back and forth across the platform, legs flashing, hair flying and bosom heaving, exhorting us to rise up against this desecration of the natural order. She stopped only to show an interminable series of slides of "this plus this plus this…" When she finally drove her pointer right through the screen, she turned, bowed low, and gave a demure curtsy. She said, "Tank you so much", and retired to a chair to restore her hair and garb to their former state.

109

It was not likely that a single soul in the room agreed with Mme. de la Brie's vilification of intergeneric breeding, which was giving us incredibly beautiful orchids by combining two, three, four or even five genera (a genus is a subdivision of a family, meaning the plants are closely to distantly related and often very different in flower forms and colors).

But there was no one, male or female, in that audience who did not feel ennobled by having witnessed a Warrior Queen rallying her troops for battle. All the men present seemed too choked up to express their feelings, but 90-year-old Jassie Pompom spoke for all of the ladies when she said to Betty, "My dear, that was me in my younger days "

Writing this some 40 years later, I can see Monique, perhaps with graying hair and a slightly less startling figure, striding about and heaping invective on the proponents of the new science of genetic engineering. Or would the idea of putting genes from a flounder into a phalaenopsis render her speechless and – horrible thought – motionless?

Exorcize Your Orchids

An old gardening guru once said to us, "Orchid growers live in a dimension Einstein never dreamed of." This seemed a bit of an exaggeration, until the famous Show and Tell program.

Show and Tell was a highlight of the MNTOS Annual Meeting. It attracted a record number of attendees who were willing to fidget through interminable and often incomprehensible committee reports in order to see how the other fellow or gal did it, grew orchids, that is. With slides and demonstrations, we were made privy to the success secrets of a bevy of inventive orchidists.

One young fellow who had won a respectable number of awards for his orchids surprised us all by revealing that he grew them in a greenhouse he had built over the outside stairs going down into his basement. Constructed of old sewer pipes and used sheets of plastic, it didn't exactly challenge the conservatory at Kew for beauty. But it had cost him less than $10 to build it, and he caused considerable consternation among fuel-impoverished greenhouse owners by remarking that he never spent a cent to heat it, since he had cut flaps in the inner cellar door that could be opened to let in just the right amount of heat from his home's furnace. Clever!

A visitor who lived on a tropical island showed us how he was able to grow orchids which required cool temperatures just a few miles from the equator. He had purchased and transported at great expense an ancient refrigeration unit which had been used by a hospital for air conditioning several buildings. The size of an army tank, this marvel of engineering cooled his large greenhouse for just a little over $100 a day. It had only one minor fault: when in operation, it emitted great shrieks and thunderclaps which had made every bird, animal and native for miles around abandon the area.

The most famous – or infamous – Show and Tell took place under the aegis of a new Program Chairwoman. Unknown to us all, P. C. Phoebe Horskall was a practitioner of the darker arts. She announced that she and two other investigators of realms beyond common knowledge would demonstrate the benefits of bringing the occult to orchids.

"Sound – the right sound – brings life," our Phoebe proclaimed. After years of arduous experimentation, she had found the right sounds for stimulating the growth of her orchids. Most effective, she said, was a steady chant that alternated "ummm-gree" with "sss-whee." The biggest flowers were produced by combining this chant with the playing at full volume of "Stars and Stripes Forever" with "Mairzee Doats."

She showed us just how it must be done, playing records on an old phonograph and conducting with a rhinestone-studded baton while ummmn-grring and sss-wheeing at the top of her voice. She was joined enthusiastically by President P and vice President Smythe, who were ever alert to new means of improving the growth of their orchids.

The next speaker had just flown in from somewhere in Eastern Europe (in a plane, though some doubted he needed one). Dr. Gorgon Spitzi-Pulonsky was garbed entirely in black, and his most distinguishing features were meticulously trimmed blue-black eyebrows which he groomed frequently with a

Madame Oriza

mustache comb, and hooded eyes which at times seemed to be an unusual shade of orange.

Dr. Spitzi-Pulonsky's specialty was Dracula orchids (yes, there is such a genus, though it is native to the Andes, not Transylvania). Dracula orchids are so-called because their flowers have sinister blood-spotted "faces" and long tails. Judging by the slides he showed, the good doctor had unusual talents for growing draculas, for no one had ever seen such robust, truly menacing specimens of *Dracula vampire*, and *Dracula bela*.

He also grew to perfection such rarities as *Zootrophion vulturiceps*, which has flowers shaped like vultures' heads. Scouring the world, he had acquired plants with charming names such as 'Macabre Marmalade', 'Voodoo Dolly', and his favorite, 'Lugosi-Loverboy'.

112

But his greatest triumph was yet to come. Dr. Spitzi-Pulonsky was interbreeding his bizarrest orchids to create a super race, which he planned to name after his hero and soulmate, Dr. Fu Manchu. 'Fu Manchu's Sneer', 'Fu Manchu's Vilest' and many other visions of loveliness would bring the orchid world to its knees in adoration. Of course, his secret method of breeding these beauties had to remain secret, but he revealed that it involved anointing pollen and pistil with a potion of certain exotic substances. While others marveled, I had a mercenary thought: here at last was someone who would take our supply of roach rumps and slug dung off our hands.

Our final speaker had been investigated by the Society for Psychical Research, reportedly with mixed results. Her card proclaimed that she was "a physic with great powers" (spelling apparently was not one of them). Garbed in green shawl and turban over cerise blouse and skirt, Madame Oriza told us she practiced her craft in a hut draped with gold cloth under the Spuyten Duyvil Bridge at Manhattan's northern tip. She was an expert in botanomancy, which means divination by means of plants. Her specialty was orchidomancy.

Madame Oriza disdained the crystal ball, relying instead on Tarot cards supplemented with a huge magnifying glass with which she peered into the "heart" of an orchid. She worked her magic with cards and glass on several orchids brought before her from the show table. Their owners were revealed to have secret sorrows or lost loves, or to be about to get raises. One orchid (its label said it belonged to President P) brought paeans of praise for its owner who, the orchid told her, was " the greatest of statesmen, destined to become the supreme leader of the orchid world."

As a dramatic finale, Madame Oriza demonstrated her power for exorcizing recalcitrant orchids. Presented with a plant that was just beginning to send up a flower spike, she fired up a bowl of foul-smelling incense and intoned an incantation which she said she had been taught by a tribe of headhunters at the headwaters of the Zambesi. After several minutes, she stood, raised her arms, and croaked, "The evil ones are gone. This orchid will bloom in sixteen days and eleven hours!" When the plant flowered (in fourteen days and nine hours), its owner had no reason to be surprised. Hadn't Madame Oriza made it all possible?

Sound The Alarm: Toll The Bells!

Anyone who grows orchids for a while knows that sloppy culture kills more orchids than any pests or diseases. The occasional bouts with slugs, snails or mealy bugs are really minor nuisances. Most dreaded are population explosions of giant cockroaches, but these are more frightening for their appearance (try looking at one through a magnifying glass) than they are damaging to the orchids.

Sometime back in the Fifties, however, some superior being declared "a plague upon your orchids." This was revealed in a vision to a MNTOS member. This gent, who habitually protected himself against germs with a cologne concocted of the strongest disinfectants known to man, alerted everyone to imminent Armageddon. The viruses were upon us.

Oh, horrors! Our orchids are doomed! Although few of our members could recall experiencing the bubonic plague in earlier lives, the new threat loomed just as large to them. Some saw a conspiracy by chrysanthemum or camellia growers to depose the orchid and crown their flowers as the monarchs of the botanical universe. An eminent MNTOS elder perceived viruses as an incarnation of The Evil One, and foresaw the end of all things. When he disappeared (actually, with the young wife of another member) more than a few were convinced of the truth of his prophecies.

A reign of terror began in many greenhouses, with blowtorch and bonfire substituting for the guillotine. The slightest blemish or deviation from perfection was a cause for hysteria. Sunburn on a leaf or aphid damage on a flower necessitated immediate destruction of the plant and all the plants around it. There were calls for quarantines, and some demanded the formation of squads of armed inspectors to pronounce judgment on all orchid collections. One dealer of dubious reputation offered to inspect greenhouses and remove infected plants, replacing them with identical but "guaranteed virus-free" plants (which naturally cost quite a bit more).

For a while, any who scoffed at the virus peril were branded as heretics and faced excommunication from MNTOS. But eventually someone took the trouble to read up on viruses. The devil viruses, it seemed, were no devils, and seldom even imps. They might cause a few blotches and splotches on leaves, and even more rarely, a distorted or discolored flower. And preventing their spread, the experts said, was easy. Transmission of a virus from one plant to another is avoided by simply swishing your cutting tool in a solution of plain old household bleach when dividing plants or cutting flowers.

Everyone breathed deep sighs of relief, and a few became known as the wise men of MNTOS because they went around crowing, "I told you so!" at every opportunity. Even Albert was relieved, though with a tinge of regret: he had seen himself getting rich replacing all the virused plants tossed out by their owners.

For the virus-obsessed, though, it was not enough. To this day, some orchid growers don masks and gowns, scrub up with strong soaps, and put on surgeon's gloves before approaching a plant. They never let themselves forget for a moment that they are the primary health care providers for their flower children.

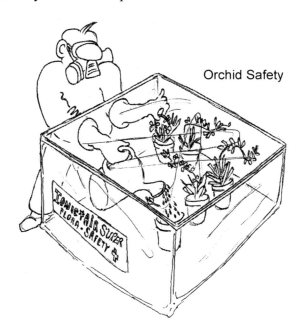

Orchid Safety

The gangster funeral

Chapter 10

The Buses are Boarding!

Some things we do in life are horrendous in the doing, but they reward us with a feeling of world class accomplishment. In our case, this feeling was most often expressed by deep sighs and an incredulous, "We got through it!"

Such is the story of our motor coach odysseys, or bus trips, if you will. They began when President P caught our eye after a meeting and summoned us with an imperious upraised finger. He approached with the air of James Bond's superior about the reveal the latest threat to world peace.

Not unexpectedly, his first words were, "I have an important job for you." We quailed, and he became majestically forceful.

"See," he snarled, his forefinger jabbing at us in classic Jimmy Cagney style, "We're all horticulturists, right? But we need to be *horticultourists*, too. We get to be good orchid growers by seeing how the other guy does it, right?"

We nodded dumbly, not daring to think what might be coming next. "So," he intoned, reverting to his Adolph Menjou persona, "I have proposed to the Board of Directors that you two become the new Tour Directors of MNTOS."

Our mouths opened, but no words came out.

"You'll do it? Good'" He beamed like an angel being given a new harp. "I'll call you next week so we can get together and discuss my ideas – yours too, of course. And remember, you'll not only be leading us to learning, you will be making it possible for your Board of Directors not to raise the dues again this year."

He bustled off, and we stared at each other. "Well, it could be fun," I ventured. "And it would get us out of the greenhouses."

Betty didn't reply, but in her eyes was that far-away look that meant she was MAKING PLANS.

The Straits of Dire

On our first tour, some 60-odd Mntossians in two buses visited half a dozen greenhouses without mishap or misfortune. Unfortunately, it was a great success.

I moan "unfortunately" because this beginner's luck emboldened us to continue, totally blind to the calamities that lie gleefully in wait for even the most vigilant tour director. Though we never flagged in our determination to "fight the good fight," adversity was equally unfailing in its resolve to thwart hopes, plans, and the most careful preparations.

Not everything was a cause for rolling the eyes and pleading for mercy. The bus company, for example, never failed us. President P had recommended a carrier he had used on cross-country tours for several of the societies he presided over, and he strongly urged us to be sure to get a certain lead driver to command our convoys.

The Conestoga Coach Company had a spotless record that began when their wagons followed the Pony Express over plains and mountains. Currently their conveyances were shining silver and red behemoths capable of floating majestically over every hill and any dale.

The gem in the Conestoga crown was their Chief Chauffeur. Here was star quality in maroon livery. Huck Minotaur combined Cary Grant elegance With Errol Flynn dash and daring. All the clichés of handsome were here – the brilliant flashing smile, blond crew cut, a neck as large as chorus girl's waist, and muscles that rippled beneath his tunic as he assisted ladies to ascend his chariot.

This gift to the female libido might well have ignited boiling jealousy in the orchid husbands, but Huck's charisma encompassed and entranced all genders equally. His smile said, "All's right with the world – and especially with you." Many a demanding horticultourist boarding for home after the last visit actually left unspoken the damning dictum so often hurled at tour leaders: "No, my every whim has not been satisfied."

Huck was most helpful at roundup time. Ten minutes before departure time from a visit, he gave one long blast on his coach's tri-tone horn. This was my signal to rush around bellowing, "The buses are boarding!" A double blast five minutes later told me to use force if necessary to dislodge the orchidist still staring as if mesmerized at a beauteous bloom, and for Betty to race into the house to snare the second-story women, the gals who used the pretext of requiring a comfort stop to check the details of the décor.

Betty said more than once that tour directors were a great untapped recourse for the Diplomatic Corps. Diplomacy and Machiavellian machinations of the highest order were vital to smooth and serene horticultouring. Seating on the buses called for scrupulous attention to the Biblical admonition to separate the sheep from the goats. Smokers must not be seated with non-smokers, snorers with non-snorers, the meek with the merry, and above all, the contentious anywhere near the disagreeable.

Always too numerous were the tourists who had to have window seats or seats in the front, middle or rear of the bus to avoid motion sickness, migraines or worse. And we must never forget to bring along certain aids, such as the special footstool required by the venerable never-miss-a-tour gent who could not get on or off the bus without its help.

Smelling salts were another essential accessory, to succor the lady afflicted with the falling disease. At least once every tour, she swooned away, invariably when an orchid became the center of attention instead of her. That her graceful faints never resulted in injury became apparent on one tour when moments after being revived she almost singlehandedly demolished a thirty-foot smorgasbord.

They say that success breeds success, but we found it much more likely to breed twitches and incoherent speech. These became permanent disabilities when we made a fatal mistake on the last tour we organized for MNTOS.

We allowed members who so desired to follow the buses in their own cars. On the awful day, we had five buses trailed by 56 cars. Local residents still talk about the biggest gangster's funeral they had ever seen sweeping past their porches. The hostess at one visit, on seeing the horde descending from their vehicles like Genghis Khan's cavalry, went into palpitations from which she still suffers today. The traffic jams drove several local policemen into early retirement, and some drivers became lost and for years were known only by "Have you seen... ?" photos on milk cartons.

The coup de grace was administered by no less a personage than Huck Minotaur. As we crawled from his bus on arrival back at home base, Huck was still smiling, but he didn't say, as he always had before, "Well done."

Strategic Planning

"The most important part of arranging any tour," President P had said, "is the survey. You must plan every step of your campaign as Austerlitz would have done. Be prepared for every contingency, guard your flanks, and keep your best maneuvers in reserve."

We gathered that what he was saying was, "It's all in the details." Planning a tour involves mind-numbing minutiae. It's not enough to find hosts who are both congenial and have orchid collection's worthy of viewing. We had to be sure there was ample parking for the buses and easy accessibility for our least vigorous horticultourists. Timing was everything; could our coaches get from Visit A to Visit B in eleven minutes, considering traffic lights, congestion at that time of day, and possible stormy weather? Were there any bridges too low or too flimsy for the buses, and would we encounter corkscrew roads with precipices on either side? Where, oh where would we have lunch? And how long, oh Lord, can we allow for each visit so that all our tourists can at least glimpse a few orchids and not offend our hosts by racing off to the next stop?

A vital weapon in the arsenal of the tour arranger is the cooperator. This person, while perhaps not having an orchid collection deserving of a visit, knows everyone in the neighborhood who does. He or she is the surveyor who maps out the possibilities, then it is up to the tour directors to check out every suggestion by personal visit.

All very pleasant, and as I kept saying, "It does get us out of the greenhouses." But it was not without its down sides. On one of various surveys, our car ended up in a gully off a washed-out mountain road, and we were chased by flocks of obviously carnivorous pet turkeys and leaned on by massive guard dogs so conscious of their sovereignty they did not feel it necessary to bare a fang.

One of our most helpful cooperators was recommended by a whispering voice on the phone which refused to identify itself. When we cautiously contacted the party suggested by the whisperer, she agreed immediately to cooperate, but also insisted on anonymity. A few days later, we received a list inscribed in exquisite calligraphy on parchment.

When we called the people on the list and told them we had been referred to them by someone who preferred to remain anonymous, the reply was invariably, "Oh, yes, of course!" Our mystification continued until one of the elegant voices on the phone revealed that she was a past president of the Grand Gardeners of America who had received its Aloysius Cuthbertson Medal for her work on the conservation of orchids.

Then everything clicked. The Grand Gardeners of America is an organization for which prestigious is a miserably inadequate adjective. Being in the Social Register is the most minor qualification for membership; a talent for giving simply super parties (with a horticultural theme, of course) was far more important.

When Betty and I donned our finest duds and haughtiest miens and ventured out to survey this tour, we were surprised to find that many of our hosts had fine orchid collections which were actually grown by their owners rather than by the ubiquitous British gardener. And whether cheery gnome or dimpled dowager, our hosts and hostesses were actually interesting people and almost eagerly hospitable.

Now, neither Betty nor I were daytime drinkers, but the day was cold and we were chilled. At every stop, our solicitous hosts plied us with spiced and spiked lemonade, bourbon on very few rocks, or "a wee bit of 111-year-old rye." When we got home, we found that our notes were completely illegible, so we had to go over the route again the next day to refresh our memories.

Goats and Rolls

One memory no amount of libation can erase is our visit to The Fuchsia Lady. High on a hilltop squatted a massive structure that was a splendid example of Early Federal Penitentiary architecture, except that it was stuccoed fuchsia from foundation to chimney.

The lady herself was resplendent in a fuchsia gown and fitted with fuchsia hair, lipstick, and eye shadow. Every wall and furnishing in the house was a shade of fuchsia: pink fuchsia, strawberry fuchsia, watermelon fuchsia, violet fuchsia, and others never seen on an artist's palette. The outdoors echoed this theme, with fuchsia-tinted gravel on the driveway, evergreens in fuchsia-bronze tones, and flowers in every fuchsia and pseudofuchsia hue imaginable.

Why, you ask, with all this beauty, didn't we include this glorious place on our tour? Well, for one thing, the lady's orchid collection consisted only of huge floppy cattleyas in (you guessed it) fuchsia colors. Also, the lady remarked to us that she was planning to redecorate the house and grounds in the new lavender and green that was all the rage in Paris.

But perhaps of more impact on our decision was Betty's muttered comment, "My God, we'd be giving our people chronic fuchsia eye."

Days of Swine and Rhodos

Only one other time did we feel compelled to pass up a tour visit. This time our regretful refusal was based on, as the lawyers say, compassionate grounds.

Arthur Biblicum was a widower about whom one wondered how any woman could leave such a man by dying. Built like the cuddliest of cherubs, Arthur had the most wrinkled, crinkled, seamed and furrowed countenance, perpetually fractured by the shyest of smiles. Although his handshake was firm, it seemed to confer the gentlest of blessings, and while he requested that everyone address him by his given name, we had the feeling that "Saint" should be appended to the Arthur.

Arthur's orchid collection consisted solely of phalaenopsis, the aptly named moth orchids (the flowers looked like, well, moths). In those days, the public had not yet discovered that "phals" could be grown in the home as house plants, and even avid orchidists were unaware of the great variety of flower colors and sizes in the genus.

Arthur had them all, from rare species with flowers of jewel size and brilliance to hybrids with leaves that stretched across his greenhouse benches and dinner plate flowers of purest white to glowing gold, crimson and purple. This was a visit our members must not miss.

Arthur suggested that his chef would be pleased to serve the tourists a luncheon of watercress sandwiches, smoked salmon, a dozen or so cheeses, iced green tea, and almond cakes. He guaranteed copious quantities that would assuage the appetites of invading regiments. We groveled in gratitude, and Arthur invited us to view his "little woodland" where the luncheon would be served.

The little woodland turned out to several acres of towering trees under-storied by thousands of rhododendrons. We were enraptured. But wait – something was wrong.

There were numerous areas where the rhododendrons appeared to have been exposed to passing glances from a flamethrower. Their leaves were brown, curled, and forlornly drooping.

"Yes, you see my problem," Arthur said mournfully. "I've had everyone here – county agents, soil scientists, the best rhododendron experts – but no one can tell me what is afflicting my rhodos."

We desperately tried to look wise, while wondering if this was a new exotic disease that could sweep through the forests and gardens of America. Strangely, our prayers for guidance were answered almost immediately.

We heard a snuffling in the underbrush. The snuffling graduated into snorts, and yes, squeals. Blithely thundering through the rhodos came a pig of magnificent proportions, followed by a throng of equally agile piglets.

"Jessica, my dear, how good to see you," Arthur cooed, patting the sow's head affectionately. His eyes lit up even more, and we shrank back even more, as a huge but slimmer swine of obviously wild boar lineage joined us. "Ah, here's Rudolph," said Arthur.

Turning to us, he added, "Can't stand creatures being cooped up. Live free even if you're not born free, that's my motto."

Having been properly introduced, the porcine family busied themselves joyfully rooting and snouting around in the rhodos.

"Should we tell him?" Betty whispered.

"Tell him that rhododendrons have very shallow roots, and any disturbance of their roots spells kaput?" I muttered back. "Can we be responsible for making him coop up these gorgeous creatures?"

The full horror of our situation dawned on us later. We simply could not subject this saint to a MNTOS visit. While all the plant doctors he had consulted had suppressed their diagnoses, we had more than a few empathy-deficient members who would have blurted out the truth and destroyed Arthur's Eden.

Feeding Frenzies

Only rarely did we have any control over the food served at a tour's luncheon break. The cooperators tended to wax ecstatic over the cuisine at certain inns or restaurants, or extol the delectables offered by certain purveyors of box lunches.

Sometimes a host or hostess insisted on victualing our tourists with home-prepared gourmet fare. One of these, a charming lady who was a vegetarian activist, served us salads so huge we wondered if the entree was secreted under them. She combined these with slabs of a glowing orange bread liberally laced with poultry grit, and a cabbage-cucumber-watermelon beverage she concocted in a butter churn.

This was quite good, but not so the herbal luncheon at the establishment known as Herbs and Orchids for Health and Beauty. Its highlights were a cold soup that one tourist described as "nasty green stuff designed to give you the Philadelphia Express," followed by meatless meatballs made with incendiary chili peppers, and a flourless bread of sawdust consistency. Desperately needed libation was provided in the form of a persimmon-grapefruit drink so sour that a single sip puckered the face for hours.

Box lunches could be lavish or barely edible. The latter was the case on a tour where our tourists had spent an exhausting morning climbing hills and fording rills to reach the greenhouses of their hosts. Much-needed sustenance was somewhat lacking in the box lunches which had been lovingly prepared at the local home for the mentally disadvantaged. Even worse, when the box lunches were delivered, there were not enough of them. It looked like Betty and I and the bus drivers would have to go hungry.

Our hostess, however, was equal to the crisis. She raided her refrigerator, and we and the drivers managed to make do with pate, cocktail shrimps, roast beef and key lime pie while our horticultourists watched enviously as they supped on their thin cheese sandwiches and dilute lemonade.

One luncheon stands out as remarkable for its culinary delights. The setting was an historic inn named for a renowned local patriot who had left the populace bereft when he stepped in front of a cannon being fired in his honor. With great dispatch, we were served fourteen kinds of hot breads, a marvelous fish chowder, crab cakes, fried chicken, spiced apples, and green beans with bacon, ending with mammoth slices of strawberry pie with whipped cream.

For once, not one of our tourists complained about the price of lunch ($4.25 per person, including gratuities). No one even grumbled when, at the end of the meal, the manager of the inn announced that a plumbing disaster had rendered the inn's rest rooms unusable. But fortunately, he had persuaded the keeper of the state fish hatchery just down the road to let us use the facilities there.

"Just down the road" proved to be nearly a quarter-mile away, but there was amazingly little grousing as our replete tourers waddled down the highway.

Viva Villa Vistoso!

It was spoken of only in whispers. We first heard about the fabulous orchid collection at the Villa Vistoso from a British guest at a MNTOS meeting.

President P invited Betty and me to join him when he welcomed Alfred Lord Herringbit at the bar downstairs before the meeting. Lord Herringbit, a blond-bearded Viking of commanding presence and lilting soprano voice, remarked that one of the highlights of his trip to the Colonies was a soiree he had attended at a little place called the Villa Vistoso. He said the Villa had one of the finest collections of orchids he had ever seen outside of Kew Gardens. Only a very few persons with titles as exalted as his own, he confided, had ever been privileged to gaze upon these orchids.

Betty and President P exchanged looks, and immediately Betty said with her most winning smile, "Your Lordship, do you think it might be possible for our Members – a very select group of them, of course – to view this wondrous collection?"

Her "you can do anything" approach did the trick. Lord Herringbit looked magnanimously thoughtful and purred, "I shall personally investigate the possibility."

Less than a week later, we received a phone call from one August "Brucie" Drewes, who identified himself as the Chief Horticultural Superintendent of the Villa Vistoso. Arrangements were made for a day and hour to make our survey visit, and we were given a password, "Orchid Pilgrims", to gain admittance at the Villa's gates.

When we arrived on the hallowed day, Brucie himself admitted us, brushing caviar off his silk tie and treading carefully on the grass in his Gucci loafers. He informed us regretfully that the owner of the Villa Vistoso, the Honorable Absalom Medvec, was in Birmingham – England, of course, not Alabama. As the emperor of exquisite plumbing, he was enlightening his overseas counterparts in the sinks-and-commodes industry on the superiority of his comfort appliances.

We stood admiring the mansion, which seemed to be constructed of some sort of pink granite in a mix of Italian and

Irish-cottage styles. At its foundation rioted masses of blazing red geraniums backed by swaths of giant privet shrubs sheared into great green candy apples. Betty said later that she had no trouble envisioning it adorned with a Hollywood camera crew and Tuesday Weld in a polka-dot bikini.

As Brucie led us across the ten-plus acres of lawn, he cautioned that absolutely no photographs were to be taken of the house or grounds. "And while no one will be permitted in the main house," he said, "I believe anyone requiring comfort facilities will find them adequate here." He opened the door to what was apparently a guest house and showed us a ballroom-size bathroom. A sloop could have been launched in the bathtub, and the faucets resembled golden maces wrested from the Huns.

We expressed appropriate awe, and a beaming Brucie escorted us down the drive to another hulking building. It bore an ornately carved sign "The Stables."

"You must see this," he said, sliding back the door to reveal a gleaming golden Rolls Royce. "I took delivery of it just this morning," he stated, and urged us to explore its gold interior. He began maniacally pushing buttons to operate its bar, vanity, telephones, music and wide-screen movie systems, and looked quite gratified when Betty exclaimed with tears in her eyes, "Oh, it's so beautiful!" (I always said she could flatter the ass off an armadillo.)

There was more to come. As we advanced through groves of dogwoods and flowering cherries, out to meet us came a herd of Angora goats. Brucie informed us solemnly, "I will see that these chaps are wearing their red velvet jackets and diamond collars when your people come."

The orchid greenhouse came next, and suffice it to say that it was a beautiful, imposing structure housing thousands of orchids of the most expensive quality, well worth viewing even if one did not get to see all the other treasures of the Villa Vistoso.

The peak of our visit came when we topped a hill at the far reaches of the estate. Before us lay a greenhouse fully an acre in size. "This," Brucie announced in ringing tones, "is the Cucurbit Conservatory."

Basking in the blazing sun was an enormous glasshouse full of gourds, or every size, color, and configuration. "The Bulgarians," Brucie stated, "pride themselves on growing the finest gourds in the world. But when Baron de Sousevich was here, the master had the pleasure of showing him and his entourage no less than 749 varieties of gourds. A really unique, and if I may say so, a superb gourd gazing party."

As we were taking our leave, Brucie acquainted us with his deepest feelings. "Many times I have thought that it is so unfortunate that we do not confer knighthoods in America. It's not just the orchids, or even those glorious goats and gourds. Mr. Medvec's contribution to beauty in the bathroom has brought comfort, and yes, joy, to so many."

We thought of the bathroom in the packing room at B&B, and couldn't help wondering why comfort and joy were so elusive to so many.

The Dismal Genius

Every tour director is entitled to one coup. Incredibly, we amassed two. The Villa Vistoso visit was one, but the other stands out because we were never able to figure out how it came about.

Jake Buckler was the mystery man of MNTOS. Month after month, he brought spectacular specimen plants to the show table. Specimen plants are extra-large, extra-vigorous and extra-flowerful examples of a species or hybrid. They merit orchidom's most coveted prize, the Award of Cultural Merit, which recognizes exceptional expertise in growing.

Jake never entered his plants for judging although he could have papered a ballroom with ACM certificates. And when anyone asked him how he grew such marvels, he only intoned, "I just let them grow."

Only once did we hear Jake speak without being spoken to. Two members were having a heated discussion on the merits of various potting media for orchids. Jake was standing nearby. The debate ceased when they realized the icon was listening. When he had their attention, he drew himself up to the limits of his Lincolnesque stature, and his eagle eyes impaled them. "Sirs," he rumbled softly, "if you know what you are doing, you can grow orchids in cigar butts."

No one had ever seen the great man's greenhouse. But this did not deter the society's female tour director. Betty had inherited a touch – more like several bushels – of stubbornness that brooked refusal from neither angel nor devil.

She simply walked up to Jake after a meeting and said, "Mr. Buckler, we want to visit your greenhouse on our June 25 tour." I cringed, but to this day she swears she detected a twinkle in the lion's eye. He said, "One o'clock. Two-hour visit. Park buses in south pasture. Refreshment will be provided." Then he turned and left.

With no invitation for a preliminary survey visit, all we could do was drive past the Buckler place. No house or greenhouse was visible from the road, but the driveway was paved so hopefully it led to well-maintained grounds. After all, rumor had it that Jake had invented a process for forging nose cones for rockets which was a couple of dollars cheaper than methods currently in use, and a manufacturer had paid him millions to keep it from falling into the hands of other nose cone makers.

On the appointed day, our buses swung into the driveway, which became a deeply rutted dirt track as soon as it was out of sight of the road. After lurching along interminably like rajahs riding stampeding elephants, we saw a small house and a huge barn. Neither appeared to have been painted since they were constructed in Colonial days. An ancient Rolls stood by the front door of the house, and a chain restrained a dog which would have made the Baskerville hound turn tail.

Jake and his equally tall and gaunt wife, both dressed in overalls, awaited us in unsmiling welcome. When all had disembarked, Jake raised one hand and signaled us to follow him, just like John Wayne leading his troop in a charge against hostiles.

Resisting an urge to gallop, we all trotted after him around the barn. As each platoon of horticultourists rounded the barn, great gasps were heard. Confronting them was a greenhouse to rival the glass pavilions of the world's most renowned botanical gardens. Though slightly smaller in size, it positively glittered. On entering, only the most stolid orchidist could stifle cries of ecstasy as he wended his way through a rainforest of great trees and giant tree ferns festooned with moss and alight with great gobs of orchids.

"Two hours?" Betty gasped. "We'll be lucky if we can get them out of here in two days" But we hadn't counted on Jake's generalship. No sheepdog could have shepherded its flock with greater precision. No one was deprived of the joy of drinking in the beauty of a single plant, yet the lines moved inexorably forward whenever Jake raised a finger.

As each awed horticultourist emerged from this wonder a sign informed one and all that restrooms were available in the barn. In honor of our visit, Jake had installed no less than ten bathrooms, each complete with bidet, vanity, and the most flattering lighting.

The promised refreshments included homemade hard cider, one sip of which sent me racing to warn the bus drivers to drink only water from the pump in the front yard. To accompany the cider, Jake's wife had baked a few thousand cupcakes. These were so yummy that our tourists demonstrated the talents of big-city pickpockets as they slipped the delectables into pockets, purses, blouses and shirts for enjoying on the way home.

On departing, Betty and I tried to express our thanks to Jake. With the nearest thing to a smile anyone had ever seen on his face, the great grower raised a hand in benediction, murmured "Pleasure," and turned and went into his house.

The Coliseum Orchid Area

Chapter 11

Nightmare in Spring

Deep in the heart of every orchidist lurks an exhibitionist. I don't mean the normal human urge to display one's manliness or pulchritude. Oh, no, it goes much farther than that.

In its most rabid manifestations, it takes the form of screams of frustration when one's prowess in acquiring and cultivating orchids is questioned. From beneath the thinnest veneer of saccharine civility, a slavering wild-eyed monster rises like a phoenix when the merits of a cherished plant are not recognized. In the homes of the worst afflicted of these orchidists, the living room wallpaper consists of award certificates, and trophies displace the TV and stereo.

Back in the days of our orchid revels, the year held only ten days for these obsessed souls. The Ides of March ushered in the supreme goal of the trophy fetishist: the International Flower Show. The doors of the Coliseum at Manhattan's Columbus Circle became the pearly gates.

The hernia was enthroned as the occupational hazard of the week as battalions of orchidists flowed into the Coliseum, bearing huge boxes, pots and tubs of plants. Baby carriages, motorcycle sidecars and ice cream carts were common conveyances for plants destined for the honor roll of orchidom.

This year, the very air had a special quality. It was composed of the usual steely-eyed determination of the award seekers, but it also vibrated with the excitement of all the little orchid society people privileged to participate in a once in-a-lifetime event.

It was the 50th Anniversary of the International Flower Show. A trophy won here really meant something. Orchid judges were coming from points across the globe to bestow supreme accolades on the worthiest flowers.

For a few, all dreams would be realized. Most of the others would experience various measures of delight or disappointment in the show. But for those who labored in the bowels of the 50th

Anniversary Flower Show, it was a nightmare to pale all other nocturnal meanderings in the nether regions.

Yes, you guessed it. This was the year Betty and I were cudgeled into service as the MNTOS Show Chairpersons. A fun job, you say? I'll let you decide that for yourself.

War Plans

Six months before the Show, the IFS Managing Director invited us to his office to discuss the details of the orchid area layout. It seemed that since MNTOS was the host society, we would have full charge of everything to do with orchids in this greatest of all shows.

Samson O'Bannon was the dapperest little man we had ever met, barely five feet tall and attired in a Savile Row suit complete with vest and gold watch on chain. His office was modeled on the War Room at the Pentagon, the only difference being that the huge maps on the walls were floor plans of the Coliseum.

"So good of you to come," he murmured. He flicked a smile at us, but we could feel his eyes taking in every detail of our persons. He offered us refreshment, but without waiting for a reply he poured us each six fingers of Irish whiskey and waved his hand elegantly toward a huge tray of canapés.

O'Bannon was not a man to waste time. He led us to a map labeled "The Orchid Area", and picked up a pointer, whipping it back and forth like a rapier.

"As you see, the main orchid gardens are in the center of the floor, here, here and here. Trade booths will occupy the perimeter of quadrants one, three and four, with a flanking movement into quadrant two. This leaves you a total of 18,614 square feet for your judging section and the orchid societies. Understood?"

We nodded, trying to look both wise and appreciative.

"Good," he said, granting us another flickering smile. "I have had copies made of these plans with the various sections marked in appropriate colors. Your duty will be to equitably and attractively apportion the territory allotted to you among the various factions and functions you control."

He stopped long enough to enjoy a long draught of Irish and stuff seven or eight canapés into his mouth. We did likewise, but before we could finish sipping and munching, he unveiled a piece of paper from his waistcoat.

He laid it on the table, and we gasped. It was a check with an impressive number of zeroes. "This is your budget, firm, non-negotiable. Any monies remaining at the end of the show will, of course, accrue to the treasury of your society."

This time it was Samson who sipped his whiskey while we gulped ours. While we were still reeling, the O'Bannon unleashed another, surprise.

He sighed, and said wistfully, "You may know that for years I was the head of the toughest trade union in the country. Now I find flowers more fulfilling. I want this to be the finest flower show ever held anywhere. I am COUNTING ON YOU."

Had we been wearing hats, we would have thrown them in the air and shouted, "Huzzah!" As it was, we just shook hands and took our leave. But we felt that we had been given a commission vital to the horticultural security of the free world.

Action Stations

The exhilaration inspired by O'Bannon lasted several weeks. We became architects and draftsmen, with rulers, T-squares and triangles working furiously to partition our Area. The judging section, we knew, had to be prominently featured, with ample aisle space for the hordes of show-goers admiring the finest examples of the finest flowers.

The space remaining required extra-cautious dividing among the societies. We figured out the total footage available, and allotted what we hoped would appear to be equal space to each society. We debated giving MNTOS, as the host society, a larger area, but since this might, as Betty put it, "Escalate the artillery barrages" between the societies, we stuck it in a corner where two quadrants met.

We unveiled all of this at a special meeting of the MNTOS Board of Directors. Our amazement, as the cliché has it, knew no bounds when it was unanimously approved. President P, Treasurer McBane and Secretary Crumquish were instructed to draft and deliver to each invited society letters of confirmation and checks based on the footage allotted to each of them.

Ah, you are saying, the worst was over. Enthusiasm was rampant, and as everyone knows, enthusiasm cannot fail to carry the day. In a sense, it eventually did, but in the meantime awaited a quagmire and quicksand, a sucking ooze of problems that demanded the painful stretching of brain cells and vocal cords.

Betty and I assumed the mentality of the besieged as we were bombarded with questions catapulted at us from all sides. It seemed that every society had just installed a new Show Chairman (for some reason, turnover in this office was extremely high). We spent hours fielding questions such as "Where the hell is the Coliseum?" and demands like "We'll need 900 free passes to the show for our members and guests."

Our nerves and tongues took on the qualities of scouring pads. Finally, with my usual brilliant mind (which someone once compared to that of a retarded chimpanzee), I devised a means of quelling the tumult.

I drafted a document, a veritable encyclopedia of flower showing. It explicated everything from the location of the Coliseum's rest rooms and hot dog stands to the timing and protocol of arriving, setting up an exhibit, and manning or womaning the information booths designed to infect the visiting public with orchiditis.

Most important of all, it stressed the warning: "In order to avoid the high costs of union labor, it is essential that all construction be prefabricated so that minimal assistance will be required for installation."

Once this masterful manual was distributed, the queriers became comparatively quiescent. We did hear that one Show Chairman had had to be replaced, having requested immediate transfer to his company's office in Zimbabwe the day after receiving the manual. But in general, we thought everything was proceeding smoothly. We crossed our fingers, legs and eyes in supplication to the Fates.

Two weeks before the show, we began to fortify ourselves with six meals a day and vats of vitamins. We knew that we would have from dawn on Wednesday until judging began early Saturday morning to get everything installed in the caverns of the Coliseum.

On The March

The great day arrived. It was set-up time. I won't bore you with trivia, such as the snow-and-ice storm which inevitably occurred as hundreds of cars and trucks lined up to enter the Coliseum. The line began shortly after midnight, and vans, trailers and ancient school buses swarmed along West 59th Street and snaked up Ninth Avenue in a haze of flakes and fumes.

Betty and I had hired a truck to bring plants for the MNTOS garden from the U.S greenhouses, and also to pick up some fancy tables and chairs Betty's father was lending the society for its membership booth; he also helped us save on hotel bills by letting us use the sofas in his apartment to catch a few hours sleep each night of the show, provided we brought along a few bushels of treats to soothe his two bull mastiffs.

The truck, which we had rented from a used-truck dealer near home, was a special joy. It had a cracked windshield, dubious brakes, and a door on the driver's side which could be opened from the inside only by lying back on the seat and vigorously kicking with both feet.

We inched our way in line for six hours, all the while monitoring both the fuel gauge and a large thermometer which told us whether or not we were supplying sufficient heat to keep our orchids alive. At last we were ready to enter the giant freight elevators which would waft us to the orchid floor – but only, of course, after we had enriched the three stevedores who hacked the ice off our truck. "Can't have a swamp up there, can we?" one declared jovially as he added a few more cracks to our windshield.

I guess we were still a little naive, because when we got out of the truck on the orchid floor expected to be greeted with at least a few smile and cheery waves. Instead, we were met by a mob whose screaming was a mix of wailing and cursing. When a few of the still coherent managed to makes their plaints understandable, I saw the problem. I raised both arms high and bellowed, "I told you to prefabricate!"

Every last one of them looked hurt. They protested that they had done just that, but it was not enough. One frazzle-haired gal moaned, "Oh, the unions, the unions."

We promised to help, and as soon as we had unloaded our truck, we began a tour. At each stop, the plaintive railings varied little.

"Three nails, just three nails, that's all I need to fasten these sections of fence together, and they're charging me a fortune for three carpenters, – one to hold the nails, one to hammer them, and one to supervise!"

"The draper draped my background, but when I asked him to stand up this divider and cover it with decorative paper, he looked horrified. He said that only the carpenters could erect a wood frame, and they needed four men to certify that it wouldn't fall over and injure someone, then I would have to sign a special overtime order for him and his assistants to come back and cover it."

"I need two spotlights on my display, but the electricians say there is a fee for plugging in each plug, and three men are necessary to check the deployment of each wire."

"They said to me, "You are demonstrating a new automatic watering system on your plants? Good God, man, you've put those pipes together yourself? We'll have to have four of our best certified plumbers take it all apart and redo all the connections. And that timer gadget will have to be installed and monitored by the electrician boys."

The litany of despair went on and on, and there was little we could do about it. Budgets melted away in a relentless rain of drive a nail here, plug in a light there. Only rarely did Betty's charm and my tears elicit a slight reduction in the number of workers or hours it took to effect these complex operations.

It was all summed up beautifully by the grandest granddame of horticulture. Mrs. R. O. Welterthwaite, who was not only one of the wealthiest but also the tallest octogenarian in existence, was the member of the MNTOS Board of Directors designated as the "observer" to oversee all things pertaining to orchids in the show.

Observing our groveling negotiations with the captains and corporals of labor, she raised a finger to us and solemnly declared, "In union is moolah."

The Blessed Event

At noon on Saturday, the show opened. We had left the Coliseum just before sunup, and enjoyed several hours of sleep before feting ourselves with a huge breakfast and a bottle of champagne. NOW, truly the worst was over.

Despite the dire predictions of weather forecasters, the day was bright and beautiful, and the lines at the ticket booths were gratifyingly long. We ascended somewhat giddily to the orchid floor, and this time we were greeted with smiles. All was right with the world, we saw. The judging had been accomplished without a single incident requiring National Guard intervention. Every exhibit was immaculate.

I suppose we were seeing it all through orchid-colored glasses. But we really felt that any imperfections lurking behind this utopia could only be mere piffles compared to what we had endured in the past weeks.

The orchid gardens were great. The largest featured a giant waterfall flanked by walls of fern-covered rocks. In trees and on boulders and hummocks blazed orchids so perfectly placed that the viewer saw new wonders of color and form with every step around the garden.

A much smaller but equally stunning garden was a patio adorned with a multitude of oncidiums, the dancing-lady orchids whose golden flowers floated on long sprays. The only jarring note was an odd little statue which everyone agreed looked like a fetus. To those in the know, it was entirely appropriate, the exhibitor being an obstetrician and his wife looking pregnant twelve months of the year.

Another, the work of a clothing designer with a scrumptious accent, displayed a host of beautiful orchids. His "Poots of Boobs" were set at various heights in beds of peat moss and separated by jagged chunks of torn steel mesh and splintered wood. Very exciting and avant-garde, but this exhibit held another fascination for us. Each morning before the show opened, we watched this exhibitor spending hours cleaning each flower, leaf and pseudobulb with a camel's hair brush, then raising clouds of dust by fluffing up the peat moss with a little rake.

We spent most of the first day going around warning our exhibitors that they must practice eternal vigilance. A moment's inattention could leave an exhibit barren, or at least disheveled. There was, for example, the myopic woman of many dimensions who we saw leaning over the guard rail to better see the beauty of a group of miniature orchids. Ever so slowly, she leaned farther and farther forward, until she avalanched onto the plants.

Thievery was rampant. Several times a day, a bold acquisitor was apprehended by guards at the exits, jubilantly lugging a plant for which he or she could not produce a receipt. And after show closing every night, a herd of Pinkertons patrolled the floor to prevent late-staying exhibitors from absconding with prized plants displayed by other exhibitors.

The Aide Who Decamped

Sometimes Betty and I had to go beyond the call of duty. Since we had overall responsibility for the Orchid Area, President P had to appoint someone to take charge of MNTOS own exhibit. As "Co-Show Chairman," he selected Vice President Smythe, who, as we all know, had a command of the English language equaled only by Lords Byron and Tennyson. V. P. Smythe promptly issued an edict:

"It is my heartfelt conviction that preparation for an endeavor of this magnitude must involve the highest degree of effort to insure the participation of every member as well as a heightened sense of unity among us all. My leadership will have as its guiding focus the goal of fostering and cultivating an eagerness to take part in this noble undertaking, and the most active and unselfish giving of time and talents by all."

Smythe backed up his gift for gab with another talent. He had a phenomenal ability to delegate responsibility to the most unsuitable persons. In charge of construction of the awesome series of decks he proposed for displaying the plants, he appointed a dainty little lady who found it trying to stir her tea. For the vital job of Information Booth Coordinator, he chose a gent whose vague manner and legendary absentmindedness had frequently forced the appointment of a designated driver to see that he got home after meetings.

This last job should have been fairly easy, for there was no lack of volunteers for the booth. It meant simply assigning two members for each three-hour period the show was open. But one morning when Betty and I were taking our usual nervous check-up jog around the Orchid Area before show time, we found the MNTOS booth deserted.

We had to take over ourselves, and for the next six lunchless and bathroomless hours we drowned in a deluge of visitors' questions. Then suddenly no less than fourteen MNTOS members appeared. All had been assigned to the next three-hour shift. We exited as gracefully as we could, and raced to a phone to call President P and dump the mess in his lap. To his credit, he handled it super-efficiently. No more problems, and he did not even charge the society for his astronomical phone bills.

In addition to being a man of many words, V.P. Smythe was a man of few actions. His one and only appearance at the show was during set-up, when he lifted a bag of mulch, screamed a most uncharacteristic four-letter word, and disappeared, clutching his lower back. He did not appear again, and he came to be known as "the little man who wasn't there whom nobody missed," One member offered to melt down a hard-won trophy to make silver bullets in case he showed up again.

Art for the Artless

One section of the Orchid Area was sacrosanct. Beyond supplying ribbons, trophies and the three walled nooks in which the orchid arrangements were displayed, we had absolutely nothing to say. This was the province of the Orchid Artistry Judging Team.

This consisted of three venerable maidens, the Misses Burleigh, Shipstone and Doreitus. Very much alike in size (portly) and garb (fur coats and bejeweled bonnets), they were nearly indistinguishable one from the other, but each exuded artistic authority worthy of the most august museum director.

One exhibitor was heard to refer to these ladies as "the three ugly witches"– (actually, "witches" was not the word used). Their word was law, and if no one could discern the criteria by which they judged the arrangements, neither did anyone ever think to challenge their judgments, except under the breath and from far, far away.

Their judging styles were a pleasure to watch. Burleigh invariably stood back, cocking her head from one side to the other to the farthest limits of her neck. Shipstone, on the other hand, had a big long-handled magnifying glass which she poked into the innermost recesses of each arrangement. Doreitus strode back and forth, snapping her head smartly with each turn, and alternately cooing and snorting.

The arrangements, to anyone enamored of the simple bouquet, were something to snort about. Here and there was a trace of taste, and incredibly a very few demonstrated that flowers could be displayed with appreciation of their beauty. Most of these few, we learned, were entries by one lady, a diminutive and incommunicative person named Dona Durkin, who was so shy she was said to wear ear plugs so she would not hear anyone speaking to her and be compelled to reply.

Dona won nary an award, for the overwhelming trend at the 50th Anniversary show was extreme avant-gardish. We saw orchids dangling from the mouths and festooning the tails of rubber alligators. One arranger took the Fort Knox approach and had giant spikes of pink cymbidiums and purple vandas rising

The Orchid Artistry Judging Team

from piles of faux ingots. Another favored the steel foundry look, using 150 pounds of metal rods, rings and gears to which she affixed dripping globs of wax that sprouted orchid flowers. Some suggested devastating auto accidents, others unsuccessful major surgery.

The most bizarre creations were given the highest awards. Best in Show went to an arrangement entitled, "The Naked Now," composed of a section of bombed-out house wall and door pitted and slashed by shrapnel but sporting orchids of the most garish hues in every crevice.

Betty and I peeked in at the judges' luncheon later that day. There sat the three ugly witches at a table set well apart from all the others. We divined that there must be an unwritten rule that mandated that there could be no mingling with the plebian arbiters of the merits of African violets, geraniums or other lower orders of plants.

Betty said that her favorite sight at the 50th Anniversary International Flower Show was the little old man who was the sole male flower arranger. He had entered a really beautiful arrangement of just three orchid flowers and a piece of driftwood on a bed of sand. It didn't win a prize, of course, but each day he came in the morning and sat on a stool staring at his creation for hours. He was, Betty said, the only true artist in a sea of schlemiels.

This took no prize.

Chapter 12

All Good Things...

Must end? Or do they really? Memories may become dream-like, and sometimes only the present is real. In our later years, we often quoted a friend who had moved across the river from Manhattan: "Hoboken is reality."

It was time to move on. This was brought home to us when we departed the Coliseum on the final night of the 50th Anniversary International Flower Show. It was after midnight, and we were unloading the furniture Betty's father had lent us in front of his house on Second Avenue. A little old lady with a raggedy-looking dog was watching. After a while, she walked up to us and said, "Dearies, I'd like to welcome you to the neighborhood:"

She was right. We were ready for a new neighborhood. We left orchids philosophically that night, and literally soon after. We went on to other – but not bigger, and never better, things.

The orchid world has prospered mightily since those days. Orchids have soared to new heights as great plants for the home as well as the greenhouse, and florists tout orchid plants instead of orchid corsages. The International Flower Show is long gone, but today hundreds of orchid shows are held each year in banks, churches, bistros and beer halls. The rose may be our national flower, but the American Orchid Society has more members than the American Rose Society.

And Birst & Borpling? Well, thanks to the genius of Albert's son (genius which said personage freely acknowledged was inherited from his Grand Old Dad), B&B is now the flagship of a conglomerate with greenhouses in 16 states, producing 22 million house plant orchids annually to feed the hunger of the new hordes of living orchidists.

Speaking of ourselves, I don't want to give you the wrong impression. We left orchids, but they didn't leave us. Very soon we realized that orchids were still growing in our heads. We scarcely ever touched a plant in reality, but daily we created perfect flowers in our minds. Our inner orchids were more beautiful than any made by nature or man. Call it mythical, mystical, maybe a little crazy, it is wonderfully satisfying.

But be aware that we reached this pinnacle of horticultural sophistication only after nearly drowning in the raging surf of the real orchid world. So let me end this cautionary tale by proclaiming an edict of my own. I know you will see it to be as priceless as any pontificated by our beloved Albert, President P, or even Vice President Smythe.

If you should be so fortunate as to be bitten by the orchid bug, welcome it. It brings a fever that never ends, aches and pains in body and wallet, and swellings and shriveling of the ego. It's also a fount of friendship, learning beyond the finest college degrees, and sometimes the purest delight in just being alive.

It will show you more of life than you may want to see, but you won't (after a while) regret a minute of it.

And besides, ORCHIDS ARE FUN.

Thomas Powell

For over forty years, Tom Powell has edited and published *The Avant Gardener,* a multi award-winning newsletter. He and his late wife Betty authored many gardening articles and books and were officers of orchid societies. They were executive and publications directors of the Horticultural Society of New York. They originated the magazine, *Orchidata,* published for many years by the Greater New York Orchid Society. In 2003 Thomas Powell was named a Fellow of the Garden Writers Association.

Betsy West

Artist Betsy West lived in New York City for many years. She earned a double Bachelor of Arts in creative writing and studio art at Hunter College. She had to argue her case to receive that degree because the art and English departments couldn't see the connection between the study of art and writing (hmmm, cartoons, print and TV advertisement, film or video). She got her Master of Fine Arts degree at Hunter in studio art in clay. Cartooning in the manner found in this book is comic relief and great fun for her, but no classes ever helped her with it.

B. B. Mackey Books

Owned and run by garden writer Betty Mackey, B. B. Mackey Books (**www.mackeybooks.com**), located near Philadelphia, is an independent press devoted to publishing horticultural books of merit and also humor.

AVANT GARDENER

America's Premier Award Winning Newsletter — Objective, Impartial, Accurate Horticultural News

Founded by Tom Powell in 1964, AVANT GARDENER has won awards for literary excellence from the Massachusetts Horticultural Society, the Garden Club of America, Bedding Plants Inc, and twice from the Garden Writers Association. Now published by Derek Fell, former director of the National Garden Bureau and winner of more awards from the Garden Writers Association than any other person, the newsletter is now supported by two test gardens: 20-acre Cedaridge Farm (zone 6), Bucks County, Pennsylvania, and Cedaridge South (zone 10), on Sanibel Island, Florida.

Please access our on-line subscription service and view a FREE SAMPLE newsletter in full color, with photography, by visiting www.avantgardener.info.

Or mail check to: Box 525 Pipersville, PA 18947

OR Box 22, Sanibel, FL 33957

12 issues of AVANT GARDENER, the full color on-line edition: $28.00

24 issues of AVANT GARDENER, the full color on-line edition: $48.00 (save $8.00)

Name..

Address...

City...................................State................Zip code...................

e-mail address...

You will receive a log-in name and password to begin your subscription.

Aphid in My Eye: Adventures in the Orchid Trade

Here is Tom Powell's boisterous account of the days when he and his wife Betty, then newlyweds, took on the world of orchid growing and showing in the late 'fifties and early 'sixties. It introduces the people who worked in the rare realm of the orchid. Tom presents the pleasures and perils of growing orchids before the days of tissue culture, battling boilers night and day to keep orchids warm, trading tales of orchid exploration in the jungle, providing blankets of orchids for gangster funerals, lecturing on orchids wherever that took them (including next to an outhouse), and the experience of overseeing thousands of raging orchid exhibitors at the largest flower show of the time. This book sheds light on what went on to bring this glorious flower to us all. List price, $14.00. 147 pages, ISBN 978-1-893443-51-8.

Copies of this and other excellent horticultural books are available from **B. B. Mackey Books, P. O. Box 475, Wayne, PA 19087.** Ask for a free booklist, or see book previews and place orders online at **www.mackeybooks.com** or at **www.amazon.com**.

Books published by B. B. Mackey Books include:

* *Fairy Gardens: A Guide to Growing an Enchanted Miniature World*, by Betty Earl.

* *Creating and Planting Garden Troughs*, by Joyce Fingerut and Rex Murfitt

* *Citrus: How to Grow and Use Citrus Fruits, Flowers, and Foliage*, by Monica Moran Brandies

* *Best of Green Space: 30 Years of Composted Columns*, by Duane Campbell

* *Questions and Answers for Deep South Gardens*, by Nellie Neal

* *Florida Gardening: The Newcomer's Survival Manual*, by Monica Moran Brandies

* *Creating and Planting Alpine Gardens*, by Rex Murfitt

CPSIA information can be obtained at www.ICGtesting.com
Printed in the USA
BVOW040601240812

298584BV00007B/62/P